Take 40 Fresh Crayfish

Take 40 Fresh Crayfish

John Coulton

To Jeff
with best wishes
John Coulton

PENGUIN BOOKS

PENGUIN BOOKS

Published By the Penguin Group
80 Strand, London WC2R 0RL, England
Penguin Putnam Inc, 375 Hudson Street, New York, New York 10014, USA
Penguin Books Australia Ltd, 250 Camberwell Road, Camberwell, Victoria 3124, Australia
Penguin Books Canada Ltd, 10 Alcorn Avenue, Toronto, Ontario, Canada M4V 3B2
Penguin Books (NZ) Ltd, Cnr Rosedale and Airborne Roads, Albany, Auckland, New Zealand
Penguin Books India (Pvt) Ltd, 11 Community Centre, Panscheel Park, New Delhi – 110 017, India
Penguin Books (South Africa) (Pty) Ltd, 24 Sturdee Avenue, Rosebank, Johannesburg 2196, South Africa

Penguin Books (South Africa) (Pty) Ltd, Registered Offices:
24 Sturdee Avenue, Rosebank, Johannesburg 2196, South Africa

First published by Penguin Books (South Africa) (Pty) Ltd 2004

Copyright © John Coulton 2004
The Acknowledgements on pages ix-x constitute an extension of this copyright notice

All rights reserved
The moral right of the author has been asserted

ISBN 0 143 02450 7

Typeset by CJH Design in 9.5/12pt News
Cover design: CJH Design
Cover reproduction: Boss Repro
Printed and bound by Interpak Books, Pietermaritzburg

Except in the United States of America, this book is sold subject to the condition that it shall not, by way of trade or otherwise, be lent resold, hired out or otherwise circulated without the publisher's prior consent in any form of binding or cover other than that in which it is published and without a similar condition including this condition being imposed on the subsequent purchaser.

To the memory of my mother and father

Contents

Acknowledgements	ix
Hors d'oeuvres	1
Memories	103
Principles	196

Acknowledgements

Food relies on the context, warmth and appreciation of friends and family, and here I have been richly served. I dedicate this journey to those who have shared so many passionate meals, and more, with me, and so have contributed to this memoir.

Especially, then, to the memory of my parents, and to Sally, Connie and Oliver; to Peter and Barbara, Mae and Theuns, Bruce and Kate, Niels and Carey, Giles and Vanessa, Sarah and Lawrence, Alain and Elaine, Ant and Mim, Sol and Marika, Jane and Nikos, Suzi and Bruno, Jean Loup and Giselle; to Gail, Warren, Coco, Marilyn, Rupert, Ivor, Rob, Penny, Oonagh, Orde, Ali and Linda.

And
To Fred, the first and last
To Linda, who shared the memories
To Lizzy Rapoo, who kept me going until I could fend for myself
To Mae and Theuns, for keeping me in the family, and for a shared passion for *essensual* food
To Peter and Barbara, for many memorable meals, and Christmas Nights
To the Widow, for the succour and sanctuary of Clogged Artery Farm
To Bruce, for egging me on

To Warren, the globe-trotting gourmet, for many sumptuous dinners

To Rupert, for high adrenalin meals in Paris

To Oliver, who knows how to throw pasta against the wall

To Dolly, Juliette, O, Simone, Clare and the rest, for enjoying Peach Whip, and other desserts

To Peter and Barbara, Gail and others who contributed recipes, particularly *The Best Soup Fish in the World*, from which the title of the book derives

To Orde and others for photographs

To Alison and her team at Penguin

Extracts from 'The Crab Feast' on pages 120 and 166 from *First Things Last* by David Malouf, © David Malouf 1981, are reproduced by permission of the author.

Photographs: pages 102, 108, 123, 165, 202, 224 by Orde; pages 135, 146, 172 by Linda; page 2 by Gail; page 140 by Oonagh. Author photograph by Rupert. All other photographs by the author.

1

HORS D'OEUVRES

The Best Fish Soup in the World

Take forty fresh crayfish. Plunge them, alive and thrashing, into very little water. When the crayfish are cooked, toss aside. You have the beginnings of the stock.

Great fish soups, really soupy stews – and often quite mediocre ones – are crowned, or bedevilled, with the sobriquet *bouillabaisse*. In its overuse, and universal prostitution, this has become synonymous with a kind of soup stew based on rockfish and vegetables in the classic French style. The superb variation on the classic that is described here, I am not calling *bouillabaisse*, since it was conjured up in the inventive mind of the Wily Widow of the Keurbooms, thousands of kilometres from Marseilles, where the Mediterranean scorpionfish lurk. The Widow does not do things by halves. It is better than any you will taste anywhere in the world.

To the crayfish stock, add (and if you are modest, you might begin here, perhaps with a couple of paltry crayfish), rockfish and a motley variety of fish heads. The vegetables are thrown in whole: bunches of leeks, celery, carrots and turnips. Liquidise three large onions, a selection of peppers of all colours, and lots of parsley. Strain out the juice and add it to the stock, reserving the pulp. Add some parsley and a generous sprinkle

Take forty fresh crayfish ...

of saffron. Then, and these are the keys to the dish, slip in a handful of dried orange slices and a bunch of fennel. Half a bottle of pleasant dry white wine, top up with water, and bubble for an hour.

Now to the magic gunge. Squeeze dry the pulp reserved from the stock juice and fry up in lots of olive oil. Let it burn and blacken. Think of the Widow in her weeds. Then throw in prawns or langoustines, swirl about in the blackened pulp, and fry. When they are done, remove and add two tins of peeled whole tomatoes, and fry up a tub of calamari. Have assembled the remainder of the fish: fifty scallops, a hundred clams, and a sackful of mussels. If you adopt the Widow's ways, there are heaving, glistening platters of everything. There may be virtue in economy, but there is certainly greater virtue in extravagance. The sense is bacchanalian.

When the stock is ready, strain it, discarding the ravaged bits of fish, and picking out bones and debris. Add the prawns, calamari, and other fish, a handful of Maldon salt, twirls of black pepper, and a dizzying glug of sherry. Let this rapturous soupy stew murmur blissfully on a low heat until the fish is cooked.

The essential point is to prepare the dish a full day in advance of its serving. The completed dish must stand for at least twenty-four hours covered in the fridge. Each time you dip your fingers in to test it, you will be overcome by the ravishing changes in depth, sensuality, and penetration of flavours as they infuse and mingle quite deliriously. The dish is presented with an aioli sauce and plenty of baguettes to plunge into the soup. We had ours on New Year's Eve, with the forty cold crayfish to whet the appetite, looking out over the mountains to distant myriad fireworks heralding the new year. They were not nearly as dazzling as the best fish soup in the world.

Early Rumbles

I grew up in Johannesburg in the days when tea would be brought to me, and my bedroom curtains opened by Lizzy Rapoo, at a quarter to seven each schoolday morning.

Her shining face retained the perpetual freshness of the nineteen-year-old who originally had come to the house in search of work, and stayed forty years. She never let me forget my role in her arrival. I was perched, aged eight, in my fortified tree house in the grand old oak which hung down over the pavement at the gate. In those days there were no walls, barbed and electrified, just a picket fence. As the stranger crossed the threshold, she was spotted by the young renegade in the tree fort.

'Go away!' came the voice of the hidden child.

Lizzy Rapoo smiled benignly at the tree.

'You mustn't talk like that! What would your mummy say?'

She had struck the right note. Her own natural kind authority, and the recognition that the *enfant terrible* in the tree was just a mummy's boy at heart.

Thus, through all the years of my childhood, 'What would you like for breakfast, old boy?' were Lizzy Rapoo's words that I woke up to.

Muttering 'Bacon sarmie', or 'Tomatoes on toast', or simply 'Poachy', I would get ready, having to catch the bus at 7.30, but always had time to enjoy what appeared on my bedside table before I rushed out. The day could hardly have begun without it.

That was the ritual for kids like me in the sixties, although mine was probably more cosseted than others. Lizzy, or 'Rap' as I fondly called her, did the same for my sister – although she would usually make do with a slice of toast or an apple – and she made the sandwiches for school, four sets in all, given that we each had to survive the pangs of Little as well as Big Break.

'Cookie', my grandmother's, and then my mother's, cook

Little Break we made do with peanut butter. Big Break, or lunch, was a more serious affair. Most days it was chicken and mayonnaise sandwiches on wholewheat bread, with lettuce, carefully wrapped in silver foil. I don't know if I was the envy of my peers, who mostly chomped burgers or Simba chips from the tuckshop (those who brought lunch revealed Marmite or red jam on thin white bread), or was resented for my superior fare. Probably the latter, as a treacherous friend confessed to me thirty years later that it was he who had sprinkled sand on my sarmies.

When I returned from the travails of school, limp, drained, and bored, there was Rap, humming quietly to herself, waiting with a gentle cup of tea, and perhaps flapjacks or a sponge cake if I was lucky. I breathed great sighs of relief to be back safe and sound in the warm bosom of Lizzy Rapoo and my mother. Rap seemed to be on the go more or less twenty-four hours a day, since I hardly had time to digest the tea before she would be slaving away over supper. We ate promptly at seven o'clock for, in the early days, the children had to be in bed by eight. The family routine revolved around us, and home was the place we felt safe and happy.

Suppers were always taken round the dinner table, however simple they might be. We were there for the communion and succour, and our closeness as a family, more than anything. We regaled our parents with the torments and achievements of school, and they were indefatigably concerned and enthralled. What they revealed to us of their days was always censored so as not to upset or disturb us. So it appeared they always had a jolly time, while only we suffered the mild pangs of school horror.

Lizzy Rapoo brought the food to the dining room, and my mother served it up. She always did the carving, my father having been put off for life by an unfortunate early experience. Fresh out from England, a simple

Yorkshire lad without airs or graces, he was asked to take up the carving at a grand dinner given by one of my godfathers, a legendary host, man of the world, and exquisite carver. The table was festooned with intimidating guests. True, natural gentleman that he was, my father rose to the carving at his host's bidding – the first time he had tried in his life – with all the care and dignity he could muster. Div took one look at the result.

'Good God,' he said.

My dad never carved again.

Lizzy Rapoo's cooking was taught to her by my mother, mainly out of her head and memories of what her mother and their old cook ('Cookie') had made. My mother had three brothers, and their household brimmed with aunts and uncles, cousins, friends and hangers-on, all eager to partake of the abundant generosity of her parents. My mother remembered the house always full of people, particularly at mealtimes, when Cookie produced endless plates of delicious home fare.

Under my mother's patient tutelage, and with a little practice, Rap took over at our house, making little variations of her own. As a robust woman – she could have been an all-in wrestler – with a natural appetite and taste for what satisfied it, she made a cheerful cook. She would taste as she went along, dipping in a finger here and there, and smacking her lips. She had an eye for the bits she liked best, so often chickens would arrive without a wing or pope's nose, and a leg of lamb with the succulent knuckle surreptitiously disposed of. Whenever I dared to remark on Rap's burgeoning girth, my mother would say, 'It's just water retention, darling.'

Thursdays and alternate Sundays were Rap's days off. She would leave the house resplendent in her shopping clothes, her faithful friend Anna from next door competing in sartorial splendour at her side. We hardly ever went to restaurants, so my mother filled in, with great gusto, it must be said. I well recall her red in the face and glowing with perspiration as she produced the Sunday lunch, always roast chickens with roast potatoes and three veg. There was a tradition of bread and gravy to finish off, with more chicken on top. My sister created a new style by supplanting the chicken with gem squash.

One of my most touching memories is the family, with noble self-sacrifice, giving up potatoes in favour of rice, simply because I developed a sporadic allergy which put me off potatoes. It is typical of my family to show solidarity in such a way, and ameliorate my loss by sharing it themselves. The tradition of the Sunday roast chickens persists to this day, although potatoes, much to everyone's relief, are now back.

There was a steady pattern to our eating habits, and everything Lizzy Rapoo made was delicious, so much more so than the dull and spartan fare served up to us by friends' mothers or cooks. Our parties were always popular and, amazingly, Rap would, with apparent nonchalance, extend the supper to feed our fifteen or twenty friends. Some came four or five times a week – Beatrice and Niels were more or less permanent residents for years – a tribute not only to the food, but to the generosity and forbearance of my parents.

Lizzy made roast chicken every other Sunday, otherwise chicken casserole, chicken à la king and chicken pie. Fish was hake in white sauce, traditional fried fish and chips, and occasionally sole (my sister's favourite). Linefish, indeed fresh fish, was unknown, something remote we occasionally heard about from far coastal regions. We seldom had beef because it was expensive, but my mother had a good relationship with Joe, the butcher on the corner, who provided a good value cut quaintly called American fillet. This we would have with all the trimmings, especially Yorkshire pudding, my dad remaining a stalwart Yorkshireman to the last, despite spending his adult life happily in South Africa.

Lamb was called mutton, and my father complained it was too chewy, but with his home-grown mint and baby potatoes it made an admirable treat. Lamb chops and stews worked. Pasta was hardly known then, except for spaghetti which was invariably bolognese ('mince and spaghetti'). Cottage pie we had (for some reason called 'Scotty Pie' in the family), lasagne, and macaroni cheese. Most suppers were accompanied by potatoes or rice with three veg: carrots, gem squash, cauliflower, pumpkin, green beans, onions or baby marrows. Salads had not yet become fashionable, and it was quite late in teenage years that any wine would accompany the meal. Lizzy's beef stew was legendary, and would always be made for my fearsome godfather Micky, last of the medieval despots in his mountain fastness at Magoebaskloof, and a great icon to me.

We ate simply but finely, with good nutrition, balance and variety. My mother was a great believer in moderation in all things, and was herself the most balanced and serene person in the world. An important element in my memory of food is having it as part of a family, with Lizzy Rapoo, in this respect, at the helm.

These days I observe my friends leading lives dislocated from their children as if the concept of family as we – and they – knew it has collapsed. Kids eke out their separate existences on pizza, chips and pastries – often takeaways – stuffed down without ceremony or relish, less nourishment, peering myopically at computer screens. They're going blind as well as anorexic. The ritual of the dinner table and the family gathering seems anachronistic. Even adults are prepared to snatch at food or take it in passing – ready-made out of the microwave by preference – as if they had no time for anything better. And they eat out much more frequently than we used to.

When I was a child, even a young adult, going to a restaurant was a treat reserved for special occasions such as birthdays. So there weren't that many in a year, and each was keenly enjoyed, ritually celebrated. My dad would put on a heroic display of generosity, insisting that we ordered what we liked, despite money being very tight in the family. It was a genuine sacrifice to splurge on a restaurant in a way that does not make sense today. I can still see my dad's wince, which he did his best to conceal, as my sister invariably ordered smoked salmon as a starter. My mother always had the grapefruit.

These days restaurants are like airport lounges or post office queues, clogged with people for whom it represents nothing special, stuffing faces and urging their cellulite children to do the same. Restaurants bulge with people you would prefer to avoid. The sense of dressing up, at least mentally, has given way, as with other cultural symbols, to a dumbed down and achingly pedestrian routine without purpose or pleasure. I recognised as a child that one could pick out the married couples in a restaurant from the sparseness of conversation – often silence – and the vacant look in the eyes. These days it applies to everyone else too.

I have to look back to recall the thrill we felt as children, which was tangible and would almost see us through to the next birthday in the family. We had an exquisite sense of anticipation, and the mounting of excitement. We dressed up and were on best behaviour. We embarrassed neither our parents nor strangers around us. We must have presented a rather touching picture, something that one has to look up in old scrapbooks to get the trace of these days.

In retrospect, the fare was hardly inspiring. Steaks (rump by preference): that was for my dad and me, although for variation my dad would sometimes give consideration to the lamb chops ('Are they tender?'). The steaks were always medium to well done, the vogue for the rare and bloody had not then surfaced. My sister would boldly take the sole (sole *meunière*; it had such a

French ring!), and my mother, parsimonious and considerate to a fault, would opt for chicken, just as we often had at home. Except, now that I think of it, she would order chicken breast, or even the Kiev which squirted thrillingly a hot rush of garlic butter, and it is these choices which no doubt made the difference, as the following anecdote makes clear.

It is one of the most endearing of my mother's confessions, and one which gives insight into her almost saintly virtues of self-sacrifice. The point is that she told it to us only towards the end of her life. In all the years, my mother insisted only on eating the wing from any chicken we shared at home. The rest of the family would polish off the best bits (my dad and I the brown meat, my sister a determinedly breast girl). Lizzy Rapoo had always devoured the neck and pope's nose, as her favourite bits, before the chicken got to the table. My mother would resist all attempts to get her to have anything but the tatty little wings. So the shock to my sister and me was profound, a mixture of admonition and admiration, when my mother confessed finally that the one bit of the chicken she couldn't stand was the wing. We took it as a sign of memory loss, and gave her the wing anyway.

Lizzy Rapoo's Stew

This is the famous dish so prized by my fearsome godfather Micky, the laird of Magoebaskloof. He claimed, in one of many shows of bravado and derring-do, to have been the heavyweight boxing champion of Westphalia, and it was perhaps in recognition of this that Lizzy Rapoo, herself no lightweight, produced the stew with alacrity and special devotedness.

Joe the butcher picked out good beef for stewing – topside is best – and it was cut and trimmed for the pot. Then Lizzy threw the pieces into a packet with flour and salt and whirled it around. The beef, with onion rings, was browned in the pot in Holsum, a strange vegetable lard with, I fear, traces of pilchard. You can as well use butter and olive oil. Herbs were not common in those days so the dish is curiously unflavoured, which is part of its retro appeal.

Carrots, celery, baby onions and sliced potatoes were added to the pot with water to cover and more salt. For Micky, Lizzy added later her jealously guarded *maroch* or wild spinach from the stash she kept under her bed. It was stewed slowly, topping up with water to keep ingredients covered, until the beef was tender. It should be simmered for as long as possible, the slower the better.

There was lashings of gravy produced in the pot and the stew was always served on slices of white bread. The expression on Micky's face as he lapped up the last drops made one think, if only for a moment, that he was as docile as a contented child.

Growing Up

My sister, whom I call Fred for reasons that will be disclosed shortly, and I inhabited a make-believe world of our own until she reached puberty in Standard Five, and discovered that there were more boys in the world than her brother. Until that dire calamity, we played in a fantasy world inhabited by Fred, who was consistently one character named, oddly, Aliz, and I was the rest of the world. I was her father, brother, boyfriend, army instuctor, school teacher, uncle, and the rulers of all the countries in our fantasy universe. So utterly absorbed were we in our reveries that my mother had the greatest difficulty, often, in summoning us to lunch or supper.

'We're in the Alizes,' we would say, and she would have the sense to leave us a few moments longer.

I don't know if dear Fred ever fully recovered from the regime, or I from my apparently schizoid personae. Fred would sit through hours of extra schoolwork under

My mother and Lizzy Rapoo with the Christmas dinner

my stern tutelage, travel with the boyfriend (Duffel King) from Athena where she lived, to Spartica, where they would disport themselves in fountains and streams (our swimming pool), struggle over the obstacle course between the compost heap and the tin roof of the shed, and complete a decathlon for her Olympic training programme before bed. All I did was make up the script and yell orders.

It went on for years, and at the time I remember us both equally engrossed. If I have any moment on my conscience, it was the time I auditioned the whole class for the choir one hot summer afternoon in our school. I sang for every imaginary member of the class in turn. Then poor Fred stood up for hers. She was the only member of the class who didn't get in.

Perhaps it was for the best that puberty struck, and liberated Fred. It left me quite desolate of course. Fred then assumed the lead in our relations, bringing a host of friends, many of them boys, to the house, all of whom I disapproved of. Our Aliz world was fractured for ever. I kept to the brooding sidelines, lamenting our loss, as Fred and her friends leapt in and out of the pool and, in time, lazed about in suncream and dark glasses, sipping first Coke, then beers and strange blue drinks out of straws. Music played – Gary Puckett and the Union Gap, Unit Four Plus Two, Barry McGuire, The Animals, Françoise Hardy ... it was a long time ago.

My parents were extremely tolerant and gracious, although my dad was sometimes constrained to shout, 'Turn that bloody noise down!' Our friends would often hang around for lunch and supper which, without so much as a thought from us, would miraculously be borne to us by the powerful arms of Lizzy Rapoo, who could juggle trays like a circus strongman. My mother must have been organising and counting in the background, and occasionally would check with us in asking, 'Are there ten or twelve of you for lunch, darling?'

We all tucked in with gusto to Lizzy Rapoo's repertoire of casseroles, stews and lasagne. I know now that these kind of dishes are very practical when it comes to unspecified and expanding numbers to feed, and that they are flexible in terms of time. Then, when we were young and heedless, we simply assumed that the food would be there, and never gave a thought to the effort of preparation and careful balancing that my mother had to go through, as well as the cost, for we were a very modest family.

We grew up in such an indulgent and carefree way. The one thing it did not satisfy was the urge to cook oneself. Everything was done for us, and we had no clue as to its genesis or execution. To boil an egg never occurred to us, and I don't think much thought was given to the distinction between doing that and producing a three course dinner of avocado soup, roast beef and vegetables, and peach melba. Cooking was something that other people did (Lizzy Rapoo and my mother), and it happened in a part of the house we rarely ventured into (the kitchen). I remember how impressed we were when our boyfriends and girlfriends rustled up a meal. Niels produced a fillet Béarnaise, and Beatrice, chicken liver pâté. These were rare and freakish moments, and we lapsed back gratefully into the familiar routine of home.

Birthdays and Christmas were celebrated in fine style. My dad would generously take us for birthday treats with a couple of friends to a restaurant for dinner. We dressed up in jackets (suede, then velvet) and ties, the girls in pretty dresses. It was an occasion, and we felt proud. My friend Chris disgraced himself one year in meticulously hacking off the asparagus tips before devouring the stalks, leaving the tips neatly arranged for the plate to be cleared.

Our family Christmas dinner was on Christmas Eve, and preparations would begin days in advance. The tree was decorated and presents arranged under it, cards strung up (about two hundred of them), and my mother and Lizzy Rapoo slaved away over the traditional Christmas dinner in the kitchen. It was almost always the family alone, except once or twice when cousins were around. Tickeys and florins (originally), then ten cent and one rand coins were stuck in the pudding, which would be set alight with due ceremony at the table. We groaned to fit it in, stuffed as we were with consommé, then turkey and ham with all the trimmings. The remains, as always, went on for a week. 'Oh no, not turkey again!'

Christmas Day we would be at it again. Fred's godparents, Dawn and Ian, held a grand lunch every year at the family home, Glenshiel, where family, friends and extended family would gather. There had to be at least twenty-two guests around the dining table, since the real highlight of the day was the cricket match after lunch on the long lawn at the big house. This was fiercely contested year in and year out, memories were long, and breaths were held in keen anticipation as the captains, David of the Doodlebugs and Ant of the Antiquarians, shrewdly selected their teams. I was always an Antiquarian, despite, or possibly in virtue of, the fact that my friend Ant had tried to drown me (perhaps inadvertently) when I couldn't swim and he could. Only the noble effort of his mother and mine, hurling themselves into the pool where I lay on the bottom spreadeagled like a starfish, saved my life.

The players ranged in age from about four (at least big enough to hold a bat) to ninety-two, when Ma Hurry led the Antiquarians in to bat. That grand old lady, like many of the more venerable players, had runners, so youngsters like Fred and me benefited from a good sprint of exercise. It was not uncommon for the match to be declared a draw as evening rolled in, and the effects of the lunch, Pimm's cups and champagne, began to take their toll. The return match the next year was eagerly awaited.

Freshers Amber Consommé

Christmas is celebrated at Fresh Woods, the farm of my great friends Peter and Barbara, on Christmas night, and it is the high point in the festive feasts. I confess, as the longest surviving guest, that I have determined not to miss it even after indulging myself on Christmas Eve and (to my shame) lunch, and it is my fervent desire that I survive to enjoy it until I am carried out feet first.

The dinner dazzles the palate and the eye. The table is glorious in damask, old silver, and rose petals from the garden. The dinner is a triumphant rendition of the traditional Christmas fare, with fatted goose, ham rolled in the Persian carpet, and pudding made a year in advance. The consommé lingers rapturously, and is certainly the best you will ever have.

Make the stock from half a dozen marrow bones, sweet and fresh, a large onion, a sprinkling of fresh tarragon and peppercorns, a generous scattering of Maldon salt, and eight mugs (two and a half litres) of water. Simmer for a couple of hours, adding a chicken (or equivalent of chicken bits) for the last hour.

Strain and allow to set. The volume will have reduced by a quarter. Skim and blot off all traces of fat.

Now to the soup. In a tall pot, put the jellied stock, a pound of minced lean beef, half a dozen chopped ripe tomatoes, some tarragon, a glass of good red wine, and the whites of two eggs, whipped to a froth.

Cook at a moderate heat, whisking with an anticlockwise motion all the time until the contents boil. Stop whisking at once, and let the froth rise to the top. Take off the heat. Put the pot back on the heat, and let the froth rise again. Do it a third time. Then turn down the heat very low, and barely simmer for half an hour or so. This repetitive ritual is vital to the final effect, since the miracle of the consommé is in the process of clarification, in which a transparent liquid emerges from the murk and gloom. It is as if clouds separate to reveal the clear ocean beneath. Only fools use eggshells to clarify.

Allow to cool and pour through a scalded jelly bag. When I asked Peter what a jelly bag was, he seemed surprised that I had not one to hand. You may use two scalded dishcloths fastened over a bowl instead. It is essential to eliminate all spots of fat. Do not be tempted to squeeze the cloths. Add salt to taste, chill, and serve in glass bowls with thin slices of lemon and fresh tarragon leaves. The consommé is a crystal clear, rose straw colour, like amber, and must be served with rose champagne. They are in perfect pellucid harmony.

Life on the Farm

We spent most holidays of my childhood on the farm in Magoebaskloof, domain of my godparents Mol and Micky. It was the most beautiful farm on the mountain, up in the mist belt, looking over the distant Soutpansberg. Being there, we owned the world. Our hearts quickened with anticipation as we turned off the tar road past Zion City of Moria, and smelt the damp rush of pine forest in our nostrils on the Veekraal road. We came up the hill through Wood Bush (on which my father once stuck in the mud and burned out the clutch), past the indigenous forest with pink ferns and the waterfall, and turned into the long farm track winding up the mountain, the majestic thatch farmhouse glowing like an impregnable bastion in the dark.

We were welcomed by dogs, servants to carry the cases, sherry and whisky for the grown-ups, cooldrinks for Fred and me. Micky awaited us brooding upstairs, often engaged in putting the finishing touches to a delicate balsawood model aeroplane that his gnarled pugilist's hands moulded with gossamer delicacy. He was

Christmas is celebrated at Fresh Woods on Christmas night

always greeted deferentially and with wariness; his moods were unpredictable and could swing violently. He once kicked a cat clean through the French windows, and could knock a man down with one club of his fist. If he began to chew a matchstick and hiss through his teeth, you knew trouble was brewing.

It was at the farm that I began to call my sister Fred, an endearment that has stuck, rather incongruously, ever since. Delight and terror were closely allied in my godfather Micky's domain, and it was sheer terror when he bellowed for servants. There was Mamabull, the cook, and Ernest and Alfred who darted about the table in white suits with red fez and sash. It was Alfred, in particular, who trembled and leapt to Micky's orders, and I felt this would be an admirable course for my sister to emulate. So I had her under training too, bawling 'ALFRED!' as I tried to get her to leap about for me. Ah, the burdens we elder siblings have to carry! It must have been due to my inflection that the '-FRED' stuck.

We ate like kings in that medieval fiefdom. Each meal of the day was a formal affair round the mahogany dining table announced by a bell and servants in attendance, although one had to dress up only for dinner. A slap-up breakfast of porridge with thick, bubbling milk brought warm to the kitchen early each morning in milkcans from the milking shed; eggs, speckled and sticky with straw, came straight from the chickens, and were normally poached in a poaching pan, the only one we'd seen outside a hotel, with rashers of bacon and sausages (no tomatoes or mushrooms: Micky would have thought those girls' stuff), and lashings of toast with the chef Mamabull's chunky marmalade. Tea was properly served in fine china with silver milk jug and sugar bowl. Servants – Alfred and Ernest – formally attired in white uniforms, fluttered to and fro, trembling always lest the tyrannical master take umbrage.

Three course lunches and dinners, and often cheese

to follow the dinner dessert. Thick, slow-brewed soups, whose heady aroma suffused the house in the mornings; hearty meat dishes and vegetables; sticky puddings with Jersey cream from the farm cows. Micky loved ripe blue cheeses, the stinkier the better. We politely declined, my father the only one brave enough to compare their pong to old socks. When there were other guests, as there often were – this was a golden age of hospitality and largesse, and many friends flocked to that generous mountain kingdom – the children would be set up at an adjacent table in the bay window. We were much relieved by this separation, where we were not directly under the scalding eye of Micky who watched what, and how, we ate like an avenging hawk. There was no question of talking with your mouth full, indeed of talking at all unless spoken to. We wiped crumbs from our lips with crackling starched linen napkins.

The terror was that we would be served something we did not like. Not that we were prissy, but our parents knew our limits and would never force us to eat what we could not stomach. The mere thought of demurring to what Micky put before us sent shudders through us. The nightmare was the prospect of steak and kidney pudding which, as one of Micky's favourites, would inevitably come round. We knew what to do. With infinite caution and disguise, we would painstakingly push each bit of kidney under a piece of crust or lettuce leaf at the side of the plate, and hope desperately that Micky had not noticed. Our noble mother valiantly distracted him with vigorous chatter. Politely, we declined second helpings – the amount of food was always prodigious – and sat holding our breaths, waiting to be excused from the table. For some reason we got away with it. Whether it was kindness or ignorance on Micky's part I don't know; I suspect he never noticed.

Before you write Micky off as an appalling despot of the old order, let me recall two anecdotes that might help to show how much I revered him, if even in fear and trembling. One night as the grown-ups dined and we children had been sent off to bed (I must have been around eight), out of curiosity I tugged a cord that dangled above my parents' bed. Immediately the house was plunged into darkness. We heard the generator way down on the farm shudder to a standstill. We heard the raucous voices round the dinner table far below grind to an abrupt halt. My blood froze. I quite believed Micky capable of pulverising me with a mighty blow. All my hopes rested on my courageous mother, who I knew would stand in his way and protect me at all costs. So when I heard only the heavy dread steps of Micky mounting the staircase, I wanted to disappear under the bedclothes and vanish forever.

His huge outline lumbered towards me like a grizzly bear in the dark. I began to stumble my apologies, 'Sorry Mick, really sorry, didn't know Mick ...'

A great calloused hand bore down on me. I shrank. It ruffled my hair, not without tenderness.

'That's all right, old boy. Good to have a sense of adventure.'

And he left.

The second incident I remember so well was some years later, when I was meant to be more grown up or, in Micky's sense, manly. He had tried taking me shooting and fishing, and I had proved useless. Even then, I could not stand the prospect of shooting a buck in the forest, blinded by the flashlight in the dark, or a coot as it quietly minded its own business in the reeds. Micky shook his head, giving up, and narrowing his eyes.

'You don't have the killer instinct, fella.'

He made it sound a dire loss. Yet, despite his own frighteningly developed killer instinct, Micky expressed delicacy when it came to the craftsmanship of building model cars and aeroplanes, on which he would expend painstaking, tender care. He collected stamps too, and would lick and stick them in the albums with infinite gentleness. He had been a racing driver who diced with Fangio in his youth, and had parachuted from aeroplanes over Crete in the war, where he claimed to have had a fling with Melina Mercouri. The acme of his model building endeavours came with his triumphant completion of an especially intricate radio-controlled glider, one of the most advanced model designs of the time, and one on which he had spent months of concentrated attention. He consigned its maiden flight to me.

I did all I could to put him off. He knew well what a wimp I was. I could hardly tell the wing from the tail. But he was insistent. It was a kind of honour. So we set off for a spot on the mountain that Micky had determined perfect for the trajectory and flight. He instructed me with exemplary patience, and had made my role as simple as possible. Cradling the magnificent model in his hands as if it were a beloved child, he said all I had to do was take it and run slowly down the slope. On his command, I should let go, thrust it gently upwards and, under the control of his radio, it would soar heavenward.

I took it with tremulous respect. I looked once at Micky as if to acknowledge his trust, and scampered down the hill. He called for me to launch the flight. I heard the pride in his voice. I let go and hurled the glider, heaven knows how, straight into the ground, where it shattered into a thousand fragments. Micky's finest achievement lay at my feet. I dropped my head in shame and confusion. There was a long, terrible silence. Then he spoke in a voice sad and soft.

'Pity, Johnny, pity.'

That's all he said. We left the mountain, and the wreck, and he never spoke of it again nor, I believe, thought the worse of me.

Comfort Chubby

I have called chicken 'chubby' for so long that my family and friends have adopted the term as quite normal. Chubby for supper, they cry. I think I got it from a brand name in Cambridge in the seventies. It has anyway a comforting, almost endearing, ring to it.

Comfort Chubby is the leader in the many chubby dishes I make. One of the greatest strengths and attractions of chicken is the wonderful variety of methods and combinations it lends itself to, making it an endlessly repeatable staple which never palls. Well, one hopes so, none more fervently than my sister and myself, since life without chubby would be for both of us unendurable.

So for comfort, particularly after a run of rich – or, worse, restaurant – food, take a good chubby and brown him in olive oil. To the pot add a glass of white wine, a handful of fresh herbs (stick some up chubby's bottom), a clove or two of garlic, a sprinkling of salt, and water to the midpoint of the thigh, and bring to the boil. Toss in a carrot, the green tops of leeks (washed well to get out the sand – nothing more irritating than grit in the teeth in mid chubby bite), an onion and a turnip. It is often best to lie chubby on his side and turn him over midway, but for this simple boiled dish it doesn't really matter.

Let chubby simmer away happily in this court bouillon, and add the vegetables in time for them to be ready when chubby is cooked. Remember to be gentle always in the cooking of chubby; he does not take to savage boiling. A soothing combination of vegetables is carrots, leeks (the white flesh) and courgettes (right at the end), all whole. During the course of cooking the liquid reduces, so what you have is the essence of chubby and vegetables in their own juices. This gravy is irresistible over bread, although I find not everyone agrees with me. I tend to rate friends according to this. I remember one being quite appalled to watch me devour six or seven slices of bread soaked in gravy as an afterthought – indeed the climax – to polishing off chubby one summer's evening on the veranda overlooking the harbour in Kalk Bay.

Life without chubby would be unendurable

Chubby with Feta and Ham

Slit the boned chubby breasts, and stuff with crumbled feta cheese and slices of good ham. Pin them together with toothpicks, and powder with salt and black pepper. Squeeze lime or lemon juice over them, and coat with beaten egg and breadcrumbs. Gently fry in olive oil, turning them over, until cooked through.

Sprinkle chopped parsley over the finished product, which will be succulent enough not to require extra sauce.

Courgette Chubby

Use a wok, that most admirable Chinese cooking pot. The design ensures that ingredients can be diversified and cooked at different rates and temperatures to capture the essential crisp bite in the food.

Slice boned chubby breasts in strips, and courgettes even finer. Start by tossing sage leaves into the smidgen of hot oil in the wok. Let them curl and crisp, but not burn. Remove and set aside. Then throw in the chubby and courgette slivers and sizzle with oreganum and several crushed garlic cloves. Swizz around the wok so that each cooks properly. At the last stage, add dashes of marsala and lemon juice with chopped chives.

Serve with the crunchy sage on top.

Armadillo Chubby

This is an amusing diversion owed to Peter. Stuff a plump chubby with Golden Delicious apples, cored and peeled, hunks of bread, nutmeg and parsley. Anoint chubby with butter and lemon juice, and season. Halve blanched almonds and insert into chubby's flesh, incising with a knife. Roast until golden brown. Then flambé in Calvados, and add cream to make a voluptuous sauce.

The Perils of Diet: Bob, Carlos, and Fred's Potato

As we grew up, inevitably, Fred had a boyfriend called Bob, who was bearable in most ways, except for his wretched diet fads. He put himself through punitive regimens on account of his high cholesterol and, like other sufferers I have known, the more he stuck to a cholesterol-free diet, the higher he zoomed up the scale. My one-time *compagno* Gianni, I recall, ate nothing but brown rice, and even cut the pope's nose and stripped the skin from boiled chicken; his cholesterol rose remorselessly. My amigo Orde's count was over the top of the scale, and doctors dismissed him with terminal shakes of the head. He rose to the challenge and devoured more prawns and crayfish than usual. His cholesterol dropped dramatically.

Perhaps it is a myth, perhaps not. All we knew was that for Bob it was a serious, not to say grim, business. Every scrap of food was evaluated cholesterol-wise, and poor Fred was dragooned into the regime. They plucked listlessly at lettuce leaves (no dressing on the salad), scraped the skin from chicken breasts, downed tubs of low-fat yogurt. Bob's levels continued to soar; Fred took to whisky. The dismal situation was made the worse by the hovering guru figure of one Carlos, who had Bob, at least, under his thrall. Carlos was possibly ninety and looked, so they told me, only about seventy-five. It hardly seemed to matter.

Carlos, diminutive, but tough and scrawny as biltong, was a ferocious taskmaster. The devotees trembled at his commands, and would happily starve for a nod of approval. When Fred felt her eye stray to the chicken thigh, she was suffused with guilt. Like the wretched Jimmy Carter, she felt she had sinned in the heart by lusting after forbidden fats.

'I will make you beautiful, like a flower,' said Carlos.

The whole dreary saga came to a head one night in Cape Town, when Fred, hip bones jutting out and pallid about the face, had temporarily escaped the clutches of Bob and his guru. Peter and I were determined to cheer her up, so took her to a farm stall which had crayfish floating in its tank. If there is one delight that Fred cannot resist, it is fresh crayfish. Or so it had been. Her face contorted with conscience and conflict, brave, deluded Fred shook her head. We urged her on. We cajoled, begged, mocked her austerity. It was as if the phantom of Carlos hovered over her shoulder.

We lost the battle. With two splendid crayfish apiece writhing in our hands, we returned to the house and produced one of the finest meals in the world, fresh crayfish live from the sea. Fred sat mournfully to one side, chomping a baked potato, without butter. That image alone was enough to make me wary about any diet regimen, however charismatic the mentor. Live and let live, remember, for tomorrow we die. For me, I'd rather keel over with a crayfish between the teeth than a baked potato.

Salads

The Perfect Cold Salad

Anyone can toss together a salad, and ruin it. The secret is to choose the ingredients with care, and make it look good. It must be a work of art: crisp, fresh and enticing, and not simply a hotchpotch. Freshness, colour and arrangement on the plate or in the bowl – indeed the plate or bowl itself – are paramount. The potential for enjoyment comes through the eye. Artistry is all.

First, it makes all the difference to have an interesting combination of greens as the base. Mere iceberg lettuce is dull, and looks limp before its time. So a combination of butter lettuce, cos, oak leaf and lollo rosso leaves, for example, together with watercress, rocket and mache makes a huge difference, not only to taste and texture, but to the look or aesthetic appeal.

Tomatoes are a standard staple – adding immeasurably to the look in virtue of colour – and they should always be firm and slightly under-ripe, never soggy or soft. I have been well trained in scouring for the perfect tomato by Linda and Mae who insist that only a perfect tomato will do, all or nothing. They would rather not eat a salad at all if the tomatoes are not right. I go along with them: there is nothing more ruinous to a salad than a soggy tomato. It is worse than a suppurating cucumber. And it is vital not to salt the tomato until seconds before the salad is served. Only then, crush Maldon over the tomatoes to bring out the sting in the taste.

The principle with salads is to keep them (relatively) simple. Do not over-complicate. Be discerning in what you add to the basic greens and tomatoes. I believe you should not add more than a further two ingredients. Here are some excellent combinations, but you can readily make up your own:

olives and anchovies
smoked chicken and papaya or red pimentos
feta cheese and olives
Gruyère cheese and smoked ham
cucumber and red onion
avocado and crisp fried bacon
smoked salmon and avocado
roast chicken rolled in home-made mayonnaise with curry powder, banana slices, granadilla pulp
grilled crispy potato wedges, chopped chives, finely sliced red onion

Once you have settled the ingredients, it is only a matter of arrangement. Let your natural artistry take over: in other words, pay attention to the way the components sit together visually in terms of colour, shape and texture. Don't waste their contribution by simply throwing them together in disarray.

The dressing crowns the salad. Again, choose one, and

don't mess it about with bits of this and that. The point of the dressing is to bring out the ingredients, to let them shine. It is not meant to be an elaborate creation in itself. So stick to the tried and trusted. Never make do with pink or other sickly combinations in bottles; they are all disgusting. Always make the dressing fresh yourself, and toss it over the salad at the last moment. Use the best ingredients you can find. The quality of olive oil, in particular, makes all the difference in the world. The best dressing is this simple one:

Olive oil and balsamic vinegar in the proportion, roughly, of six to one, with a crush of Maldon, twist of black pepper and a smidgen of crushed garlic; if you like, a touch of Dijon mustard and/or fresh lime. French tarragon wine vinegar is also excellent as a change from balsamic.

The proportion is a matter of taste and you need to stick your finger in to tell. A delicate sprinkling of fresh herbs such as tarragon, chervil, basil, borage, lovage, dill or thyme in the salad is always good. Don't overdo it, and steer clear of dominating tastes such as rosemary, sage or marjoram.

Mix the dressing well and throw generously over the salad shortly before serving. Toss the salad so that the dressing permeates at the table, once everyone has had a chance to admire the presentation. If it looks beautiful, it will taste beautiful.

Warm & Cold Salads

There is great scope for variety and innovation in combining cooked ingredients, still warm, to a basic cold salad.

Warm Chicken Liver Salad

Take a handful of chicken livers and peel away the veinous strands. Salt and pepper them and toss whole into a pan lightly smeared with olive oil, to which add a sprinkle of Chinese Five Spice Powder and a dash of red wine. Cook until the livers are still pink in the middle.

Add the livers to a basic salad of greens and tomatoes, and dress. This salad is even more delicious with duck liver.

Goat's Cheese Salad

Goat's cheeses range from the acrid blue to the creamy mild. Some are good for cooking, and they give a luscious bite to a salad. It is best to grill slices of the cheese on bite-size slivers of baguette. The cheese melts into the now lightly toasted bread. These slices are dropped into your basic salad, and give it a good crunch.

Green Bean Salad

French green beans (*haricots verts*) are distinguished by their delicacy. They are slender, in contrast to the gross chewy beans ordinarily found. Avoid these for a salad, where the beans are blanched until *al dente*. They must be crisp to the bite, never soggy.

I find such beans always an admirable alternative, even supplement, to salad greens. They go well with tuna and feta cheese.

Asparagus Salad

The best way to cook asparagus is grilled or baked in the oven, splashed with olive oil, Maldon, and parmesan cheese. All that finicking business of balancing them in a pot to steam while keeping the tips clear of the water (perhaps capped in silver paper) is an unnecessary bind, and they often turn out overcooked, or with the tips still raw. In the oven, they bake to a firm consistency, and should be removed before they get too soft. The parmesan melted into the asparagus is delicious, and the sauce resulting from the combination should also be added to the salad.

In my view, asparagus are so special in themselves, and their season so limited, that they are best savoured on their own, ideally smothered in hollandaise sauce. But added warm to a salad they give extra lustre. Grate shavings of parmesan over them. I recall happy days picking the new purple shoots bursting from the ground at a farm outside Oxford in the early summer.

Baby Calamari Salad

Douse the pink shell-like calamari in olive oil, paprika, Maldon and pepper, and toss over a hot skillet for a few sizzling seconds. Throw it over rocket, radicchio, finely shredded red peppers, and swirl with a mixture of wholegrain mustard, olive oil, lemon juice, a crushed garlic clove, Maldon and black pepper. Serve with thick chunks of soda bread.

Passing Time

Time passed. It tends to do that. And the old truth hammered in by parents and older people that it speeds up is seldom heeded until too late: the moment we turn round and exclaim, where did it all go? – as if we haven't really been all there. In truth, we haven't, and it is an absence we live to regret, when we no longer have the prospect of making up for lost time. I have been haunted by the passing of time and intimations of mortality from an early age. It might explain something of the restlessness of my life, in limbo more than anywhere else, the anathema of settling down, becoming comfortable, content, and – God save me – *normal*.

With passing time, things happened, not unusually. I left school behind, slotted into university, went on to Cambridge, saw a bit of the world. It was at Cambridge that I first took an interest in food, and started to cook for myself. I had to adapt to life without my mother's home cooking and Lizzy Rapoo. Food in College was pretty execrable and my supervisor Michael, a rebel himself, was only too happy to be taken to restaurants, and in a couple of years I had been to more than in my life until then. Warren, my globe-trotting American friend, often jetted in, and always treated me to fabulous dinners. I cooked at Leckhampton, where I had a graduate student's room that led into the rose garden, mainly enticing dishes for Oonagh who surreptitiously spent each weekend with me, much to the wrath of Jaggard the fearsome porter (straight out of *Porterhouse Blue*). The readily seductive staples are asparagus, smoked salmon and oysters, all of which hardly require a chef's touch. I ventured into pasta, veal dishes, chubby of course (that was when the name originated) and an exotic Jerusalem artichoke soup, for which Oonagh rather touchingly still has the recipe. I like to think it's because the soup was that good.

The lamentable day came when I had to start working. University, of course, is not work; never believe any student who claims so, unless they are extremely stupid. I worked in broadcasting and early days of television, I wrote reviews for magazines and papers, even on restaurants, and I lectured at universities some dim, and some astonishingly receptive, students. I finally found the brightest and most beautiful, Linda, and married her. We took the plunge and set off in search of a dream future somewhere else.

It is a dispiriting exercise to venture out boldly to explore new worlds, only to realise they are no better than the one left behind. When the great, tragic Tolstoy's body was found slumped and frozen at the railway station outside his village, the last note scribbled by this staunch icon of fortitude and moral resolve read: *Everything is the same, worse even.* It is a devastating *aperçu*, and one, incidentally, that I have often used to dampening effect in speeches at wedding and birthday occasions. It is surprising that I am still invited at all.

As those old Greeks remind us: Do you imagine you are the only one to have had this experience? Though you cross the boundless ocean, you will be pursued by your failings. How can you wonder your travels do you no good, when you carry yourself around with you? You are saddled with the very thing that drove you away.

Linda and I embarked on the great adventure of crossing the boundless ocean to see what lay beyond. Of course we took ourselves along with us – hard as we tried not to – but we were to discover great differences, broad horizons and deep satisfactions. The only error was to start where we did, in England, believing that familiarity would be less traumatic than adventure. Always a mistake. The only familiar element in England was the language, even if we could hardly decipher any of the accents. We seemed to speak English, they a kind of gobbledegook. Perhaps it was the weather.

We quickly set it to rights and changed course, but it is almost true to say that we gave up trying to live in England mainly on account of the food. We simply had to look at the people to see what they ate. Surveying a shopping trolley was instant vomit. As we despondently realised, life was bearable as long as we ignored the weather, the people and the food. It came as some consolation to hear that a questionnaire, directed at English expatriates on what they missed most living abroad, invariably elicited the answer: *France!*

So we took the cue, and whisked ourselves across the Channel. It is extraordinary how instant is the transformation. The moment we hit French soil, right in the hovercraft precinct, we did wheelies of delight in the car before driving away deliriously on the wrong side of the road. All roads lead to Paris.

Fillet of Veal

People who live in England can seldom afford veal. It is another measure of the dreariness of their lives. Also, being England, there is a prissy moralistic aversion, not only to the price, but to the animal itself. This is no more than a hypocrisy of squeamishness.

It is perhaps worth a word on this subject. For a people who manage to stuff down black pudding, calves' brains, haggis, and the euphemistically named sweetbreads, to wrinkle their noses at the prospect of a baby cow, is of course no more than a reflection on the fabled English expertise in double standards.

The noble (at least in matters culinary) French, by refreshing contrast, have no conscience, indeed no word for squeamish. There is, importantly, a sense of discrimination that nevertheless holds them in reasonable check, and sets a limit, an index of decency it might be said. I believe they have a balance pretty well ingrained in the culture of food. Thus they will attack most foods with unabashed relish, but draw the line way before the Japanese and other Orientals.

These err on the opposite side to the English, perhaps. Where the English are queasy and moralistic (although without consistency), the Oriental knows no limits and has no shame. He is an indiscriminate predator.

If, by any chance, my argument seems prejudiced, think only what kind of human being it is that will slaughter a Bengal tiger for its penis, a rhinoceros for its horn, and a monkey (alive) for a scoop of its boiling brain.

Here, I believe, we have a quality distinction – one that reflects on human values – which is a cut above the relativity debates surrounding cows, eels and piglets. These might be debated endlessly.

So to the veal which, after all, is only a young cow. Cows, unless you are a Hindu, are made to be eaten. There is no reason to suppose that the young should not be more desirable and succulent than the old; this is a truth easily assimilated in human terms. Thus to parade a juicy and tender fillet of veal is one of the great allures to culinary satisfaction.

It should be cooked slowly, with the reverence accorded to the young, particularly those who die young. A Keats or a Schubert of a dish! Treat it with simplicity. Dust with fresh herbs, seal in olive oil, and simmer in good white wine and herbs, perhaps with a touch of garlic. This rustic French mode is all that is required to bring out the natural succulence of the beast. It sings through the senses, and melts in the mouth like a lover's kiss.

A Parisian Affair

Paris is the most romantic city in the world, of course for lovers, and for lovers of food. Every nook and cranny – and, despite the grandeur of design, there is an endlessly discoverable variety of hidden secrets and subtleties – pullulates with sexuality. It is in the scent of the river, and the roses, and the dogshit. It is in the garlic on the breath, and the Gauloises, and the acrid stench of gutters and old stones. Parisians rightly believe that one cannot have beauty and radiance without the dark, corrupt undercurrent, that *les roses* emerge from *la merde*. To step in it – and in Paris the streets are thick and slithery with dogshit – is a sign of luck. *C'est normale!*

It was here that I really began to notice, and nurture, the idea of food. I came from a rather retarded background, food-wise, having been spoilt by the indulgences of family and Lizzy Rapoo. I had never really cooked – never really had to – and it took the heady stimulation of Paris, and the admirable French food ethos, to goad my salivary glands into action. I started experimentally, and with great relish, and was surprised to find how readily I coped. I learned quickly that there is not nearly as much mystique in food as appears from the outside. All I needed to do was follow my nose, literally, and trust

Paris is the most romantic city in the world

my palate; yes, and dare to plunge in. When it comes to food, there is no better injunction than to live dangerously. I dived in, and found to my amazement that I could swim.

Linda and I stayed in rue du Cherche Midi in the chic heart of the Left Bank. We lived with Linda's sister Mae, and it was sheer indulgence from the first croissant of the morning to the last espresso of the night. Linda modelled for fashion magazines, and her face adorned every street corner in Paris. Mae and I would accost strangers, gesticulating proudly, *Ma femme! Ma soeur!*

We were by no means inured to the sexual allure of the city, indeed one would have to be blind to miss it. It is everywhere. The people radiate it. Their faces betray it. Their style expresses it. The lingerie shops, boutiques, fashion emporia, advertising billboards, magazine stalls, sex shops, street tarts. It is in the contours of buildings and bridges, the flow of the river, the statues in the gardens. It is in the sad smile of the clown, and the sultry eyes of the fire-eater. The city is made of sex, and of course it beams from every shop window, and every restaurant, showing off its food. Food, too, is sex.

There is a boggling gluttony of sexual appetite. It almost stops the heart, and if sufficiently indulged, surely would. *Épiceries, boulangeries, pâtisseries, boucheries, poissonneries, fromageries, crêperies, crèmeries, charcuteries, chocolateries* . . . there is a name for every variety and nuance of food shop. There are hideous supermarkets sprouting everywhere, a late and regrettable American-style aberration in France. The true glory lies in the individual specialists, the culinary artists. For the food lover, the excitement of discovery, the real adventure, lies there too. Every street is festooned with bounty, and each area has its differences and specialities.

We plotted our meanders through the city in search of food markets. They are everywhere, and each has its distinction. There is no more encouraging enticement to cook than scouring the markets, overwhelmed by aromas and artistry. The highly sophisticated transport network, road and rail, is geared to speeding foodstuffs from every corner of the country to the capital. All through the night, trains and trucks are hurtling towards the centre, bursting with food to fill the ravening belly of the city. Paris is, above all, the culinary capital of the country.

We got to know where to find the most shimmering *coquilles*, the plumpest quails, the exotic spices, the most glittering raspberries and figs. Breads and cheeses and pâtés and brioches, we tried them all. Then the *pâtisseries* with their irresistible decadence in tarts, cakes and pastries, wickedly disguised as works of beguiling artistry. It is surprising we did not collapse. We ate all day long it seemed, then rested up to begin again at night. It was an endlessly diverting ritual, and we seldom repeated ourselves. That in itself is tribute to the infinite variety and stimulation that characterises the food of Paris. Finally, bloated and exhausted, we'd keel over and play mah-jong long into the night, Serge Gainsbourg croaking away, Russian vodka iced from the freezer.

The great contribution of France to the world is that it has given us our vocabulary of sex and food, each rooted in passion. There is nothing like making love in French, or with a French lover, or even in France. A French kiss is the beginning of a lifetime addiction, French knickers of a lifetime affair. The French have lovers and mistresses, not wives; they have *affaires* before, after, and within, marriages. A French *bistrot*, *brasserie* or, indeed, *restaurant*, piques appetite for food. The word *pique* itself does it. When they say *ooh-la-la*, you know they mean it. Our food fantasies, as much as our sexual ones, are French. Our pleasures derive from their inspiration.

One has only to sit at a café sipping a *café crème*, or with a glass of *pastis* at one's fingertips, to have a vignette on the world that fulfils all fantasies. Cafés exist for the sense of living theatre: you are sitting there to see and to be seen. That is why you linger for hours over your drink, and why you order another. You will never be hurried away, the life of the café revolves around you. Before you there is a perpetual flow of drama, pleasure and, always, sexual frisson. The scent of sex on the air is as pungent as food, and mingles with the Gauloises and perfumes. The waiter puts the plate of *steak frites* before you. There is a girl in the street eating fire, another flaunting the peach swell of her *derrière* as she glides by, and, that night, as you will never forget, the silhouette behind the transparent drapery of a second floor window of a figure, casually pulling off her top over her head, and stepping out of her jeans, naked, unabashed, and smiling at her reflection in the mirror.

We concocted hundreds of glorious meals, often just for the three of us, falling back in a glow of radiant contentment as yet another duck, pheasant, partridge, quail or chubby – not to mention lamb, cow, calf, pig, and half the fish of the Mediterranean – nobly sacrificed itself for our rapturous palates and burgeoning stomachs. Then the cheeses ... then the desserts ... and the wines, the cognac, armagnac. It was quite exhausting to keep it up. We enjoyed fine dinners, parties and restaurants with our Parisian friends, Jane and Nikos, Suzi and Bruno (whose magical Japanese forest wedding, resplendent with Shinto shrine, was a supremely sensuous experience), Lynn and Olivier, Claudine, and a stream of visitors and guests. We felt the idyll should go on for ever, or until we burst.

Yet, yet ... *Alors!* When a man is tired of Paris, he is truly tired of life. And there comes a point where, however passionate one's love, Paris turns. One suddenly cannot abide, *for one moment longer*, the sallow complexions, the avaricious gleam, the stinking beggar, the groaning platters. Even the dogshit repels.

It is a curious and disconcerting transition, for one's attachment is primary, visceral, in the heart and the gut. What one moment before enchanted, tempted and seduced, now drives one away. One more duck *confit* would kill one, one more *mannequin* swinging her sweet *derrière* will make one slap her, one more *fleuriste* plucking a rose will drive one to suicide. The romance of the place turns to anger and disgust. All that indulgence, pretension, superficiality! *Arrêt! C'est suffit!*

This is a phenomenon familiar not only to the capricious visitor, but to Parisians too. It is the dichotomy they recognise, and love to hate. They, of course, have a permanent cynical carapace, a mask that understands all but forgives nothing, yet even that cracks. On the very first day of the summer holidays every Parisian is on the *autoroute du soleil*, in search not only of the sun, but of escape from the claustrophobia of the city. It is unremitting. Paris never sleeps, and the unabated cascade of noise and frenetic disruption from cars, hooters, police sirens in particular, yells, screams and ejaculations, drives one to distraction, or murder.

One sees enactments of the disenchantment, sometimes violent, sometimes capricious. The city is, after all, a theatre, a showpiece for the whole gamut of human emotions. Paris is a passionate heart, and passions are unpredictable. I've seen a stabbing on the street, occasioned by no more than a hoot at the wrong moment when the summer temperature was too steamy. I watched two girls in miniskirts (and a Mini) bring the traffic to a standstill, simply to satisfy a lust for a crêpe. So they stopped in the middle of the busy road, were flirtatiously chatted up by passing boys on motorbikes, nonchalantly strolled to the *crêperie*, slowly broke the crêpe in two, and relished it between them as the cars behind went crazy.

It is a manifestation of the *Fuck You* attitude that characterises Paris, and, to my mind, with good justification. It is a symptom of the pride and passion, the fierce individuality of its citizens, and the beauty of their city. They did not come through *la Révolution* for nothing. There is, of course, a delightful hypocrisy here, in a people who could hardly be more elitist, chauvinistic, superior, and xenophobic. Naturally that does not mean they should put up with crap from *touristes*, American or German riff-raff. It is bad enough if one comes from the provinces. It is an amusing spectacle to watch a policeman crumple his face in disdain as a tourist, stabbing at a map, asks him where to find the Eiffel Tower. You can see it over his left shoulder. The cop shrugs and walks away, as if he has never heard of such a ridiculous thing. The Parisians are the most *chic*, sexy and arrogant people in the world, and that is their charm.

A word on the arrogance of waiters, sometimes bemoaned by the whimpering classes who have to find reasons to resent what they can never emulate. To me, the arrogance of waiters, in line with that of the Parisians' *tout court*, is one of the virtues and charms that draws one to Paris time and again.

We need to understand that to a Frenchman there is nothing servile about a waiter. He is an equal *citoyen*, a professional, and we are on his turf. The waiter makes the rules, and one almost cringes with gratitude to be there. Call him *garçon* and see what happens. You will get your plate of *moules* in your lap, your *vin rouge* cracked over your skull. He is not a boy, any more than you are a barbarian. There is nothing as abject these days, under the lash of declining tourism and European Union political correctness, as a Parisian waiter desperately struggling with your language, trying to please, smiling ingratiatingly, and not giving offence. It quite robs the experience of its charm.

I was distressed to see the other evening at the Café de Flore, one of the famous, now shamelessly tourist, bistrots where Sartre and friends once rubbed their bottoms on the faux wicker seats while groping for the meaning of life, waiters posing abjectly with capering Japanese tourists flashing digital cameras. It signified the end of an era. I must revert to the Deux Magots next door for a resuscitating burst of traditional waiter arrogance.

Duck Breasts

The French have an admirable attitude to food. Every market and village street pullulates with animals in every conceivable state of dismemberment. The spectacle is a wonderful appetiser.

Thus geese are fattened, the livers one of the great glories, and ducks are bred with irresistibly plump and succulent breasts. They say, even with the exquisite delicacy that my godfather Micky brought to the art of carving, that duck is perhaps too much for two and too little for three. At Fresh Woods, a second duck would always be served specially for me. Not necessary with the French duck, where the breasts are the size of fillet steaks.

Pan fry the breasts whole, sprinkled with Maldon and black pepper. Keep turning until they are almost, but not quite, cooked through. They are then ready. The French have duck as rare as beef, that is, very rare indeed, so how well done is up to you. My preference is on the medium side of medium rare, pink but not too pink.

You can add what you fancy to the juices in the pan. A swirl of cream is always tempting, not usual with duck which can be rich, but here the breasts are deliciously lean. Put together with spices or herbs as you choose. You might even set the breast alight with a splash of brandy. Or try a dash of cassis, that elixir of blackcurrants which, when splashed into wine, makes the perfect preprandial aperitif. The sweet fruitiness is particularly fine with duck.

Happily, these jolly ducks are reared locally from French Barbary stock, which has been bred to eliminate discoloration from the flesh. They are plump and pink. Prepare for a revelation.

Duck with Nectarines

Stuff the duck with three nectarines, skinned and chopped, brown breadcrumbs, an onion, a pinch or two of nutmeg, zest of lemon, a handful of crushed walnuts and lots of mint. Bind with an egg.

Prick the duck all over, and roast on a grid above the roasting tray so that the fat drips off. The element that ruins duck most often is the overwhelming taste of fat, so get rid of as much as possible in the roasting.

For the sauce, skim off most of the fat from the roasting tray, and over a good heat add flour to absorb the juices, squeeze in the juice and pulp of a nectarine, add stock if you have it, season, and sieve until the sauce is clear.

Duck with Figs

Some time back, one could only find duck that had been reared by the nuns on milk, or so we believed. They were a rarity, and the delicacy of the nuns' soothing hands extended to the way we cooked them.

One of the best combinations was with fresh figs, purple and splitting at the seams. Stuff the duck with as many as you can shove inside, and roast on a grid over a basting tray so that the fat drips off. When the thigh juices run clear, the duck is done. For the sauce, strain off the fat in the tray and reserve the juices. Add some mashed figs and a dash of liquor, which might be brandy (in which case flambé), or a sweet fruit liqueur such as Van der Hum. Smother the duck in this sensual syrup.

Country Pleasures

Finally, inevitably, the day came when we had to get out of Paris. We hit the southern route to the sun, car loaded to the brim with all our worldly goods, and landed up in

*Each village is unique, and forms a tradition in food
that is proud, competitive and strong*

Vaison-la-Romaine, a Roman jewel in the Vaucluse, in Provence. There, on the hillock above the town, we were cloistered in a medieval fortified farm, once the seat of Knights Templar, with the gashes of their insignia faintly visible on the stucco. We had a haunted chapel, vines and olive groves, lavender, tall cypresses and Van Gogh plane trees. Across the Roman bridge that had withstood the flood which ripped the town in half days before we arrived – *la force de la nature!* – a marketplace that dazzled the senses. We had lunch in the café next to the fountain, faded crumbling facades, savouring our bulging baskets.

This was Peter Mayle country. The cows, sheep, pigs and goats, the grasses and roots they feed on, the soil that nurtures, the flowers, herbs, and blossoms that fall, the river running through, perhaps even the direction the wind blows and where the sun rises: each element in the natural pattern makes a subtle impression on each place's contribution to the culture of food. It makes each district, town and village in France unique, and forms a tradition in food that is proud, competitive, and strong as blood.

We had never imagined cheeses of such organic shapes, hues, aromas, tastes, and freshness glowing from the vats. Cheese is truly the major contribution of France to the culture of food, and the great cheeses are regarded with a reverence that outstrips everything else in the marketplace, and are consumed with the finest wines that do them justice.

Flesh, fish and fowl: plump duck breasts, quails and pigeons and pheasants; rosy salmon, eel, swordfish sparkling from the sea and rivers; lamb, veal, beef and pork filleted and parcelled with the finesse of artists. Rabbits, deer, wild boar from the forests. Weird and psychedelic mushrooms. The voluptuous contours of apricots, melons, peaches and pears. Twenty varieties of salad leaves and lettuces, twenty shades of green. Bright tomatoes, beans, courgettes and peppers. The air hazy with the scents of herbs: rosemary, thyme, basil, tarragon; great bundles of plaited garlic, fat and purple. Olive oils, as strictly controlled and calibrated as noble wines and as highly prized, golden and green and fragrant. Breads contorted for every occasion, studded with olives and nuts. And the *pâtisseries*! I am not a pudding man, but the astonishing delicacy and audacity of the pastries, tarts and flans made one salivate, not only the palate, but the eye for artistry. Sausages, cold meats, tapenades, pâtés, foie gras, everything that can be pickled, preserved and plucked, rose like phoenixes to delight and astonish each new market day.

One of the rarest pleasures is to find, indeed savour, the elusive truffle. I have sought them out with a passion. The first was a truffle omelette at the famous restaurant at Mont St Michel. The sliver was so measly, and the price so exorbitant, that I felt resentful and ripped off. Much better at an unpretentious *routier* café in the countryside, where truffles might be spontaneously thrown into the *daube*, or a discreet family restaurant tucked next to the old watermill in a village only you can find.

Best of all, seek them out yourself at a country market in the autumn, bear them away like the sacred black gold they are, and savour them slice by slice in any stew, soup, omelette or soufflé you create. The faintest suggestion lends a penetration and pungency to the dish that lingers through many a long autumnal night. As with all rare and expensive things, there is a lively trade in skulduggery when it comes to truffles and the unwary foreigner. *Caveat emptor.*

Traditionally, truffles are rooted out by pigs, which have a voracious nose for them. Men hurtle through the oak woods of Périgord, attached to pigs on ropes, ferociously pummelling the ground. The only way to save the truffle is to strike the pig a mighty blow to the head

Jean Loup and Giselle, lovers of simple life

with a stout stick, and snatch the truffle while the pig lies comatose among the leaves. This is strenuous work, not without risk, so these days dogs are trained to do the job, and the truncheon is left at home.

I had met a truffle hunter in Turkey. The odd thing was that one could identify what he did by one look at his face, or at least his nose. You could not miss it, snout rather than nose, pig rather than man. It was pink, hairy, nostrils distended, radiating the odour of festering oak. His eyes were wizened, truffle-dark, and he snuffled as he spoke. He was illiterate and half mad, but he made himself rich in the village. When he wasn't snuffling truffles, he crept into the woods on dark nights and shot swans with a bow and arrow. He was a thoroughly disgusting creature.

Jean Loup, our delightful friend in Vaison, is a natural man, and a lover of simple life. He used to make mannequins for fashion houses in Paris, but prefers being a peasant in Provence. He still sculpts, and picks peaches in the summer and grapes in autumn. He owns nothing of material value, it is all within, and he is rich beyond richness. It was bliss to sit in the village square under the trees, with the fountain spurting, drinking *pastis* and hearing Jean Loup's fiery tales and infectious laughter. When the band played, he scooped Giselle into his arms, a wife twenty years his senior and filled with the same ebullience and sensual spirit, and danced like a prince.

He told us of a friend who inherited a small strip of land from an aunt. It was all he had in the world, and he could never make ends meet. On the land were a cluster of oaks, and the man had a pig. The rest is history. One can never tell where truffles will turn up, how many, or for how long. Jean Loup's friend literally struck a gold mine, the best source of truffles in the Vaucluse. The peasant became a truffle millionaire. I wished it had been Jean Loup himself.

The French idyll lasted for years, the most resplendent

Country pleasures: lunch at our mas in Vaison

imaginable. We scoured the country like rampant, virgin hunters in search of stimulation and satiation, epicurean delight. We ate our way through most of the departments of that ravishing country. How we did not burst, in a *grande bouffe*, was a miraculous testimony to our hardihood and resilience. But, like all magical things, even France had to end. We put it off as long as we could, then traipsed homeward, hearts and palates agog with memories, and knuckled down to work. We made a terrible mistake. We opened a restaurant.

Quail with Fennel

I keep having to slap my nephew Oliver (with the sticky wooden spoon) when he whinges that quail are wildlife and therefore off bounds, stamping his foot with the indignation of youthful fervour. I respect greatly the little fellow's passion for *la vie sauvage*, even his concomitant conviction that the human race is worthy only of extermination. I asked whether he included himself (and, with slightly more hesitation, myself), and was not greatly comforted by his cheerful assent. There was some consolation in his assuring me that I would be the last to go, just before himself.

But to return to the quail. Uneatable by principle perhaps, certainly not inedible. These toothsome little birds with their plump thighs (something of Naas Botha in the thigh) are not as frail and unsatisfying as they appear. There is flesh on them bones, breasts as well as thighs. I think even my noble mother might eschew the wings.

As consolation to Ollie, the ones we get are bred in captivity, thus neither they nor he should be surprised that they end up in the human belly. They arrive on the shelf hunched up whole like plucked mice, or flattened as though run over. Do not be put off. Remember *Babette's Feast*, that incomparably fine tribute to the art of cooking, as much as to the art of life, where the quail are incarcerated in pastry, only their beady eyes protruding, somewhat accusingly perhaps, through the crust. They present an irresistibly appetising temptation.

Two quails each is very filling. Sprinkle them with olive oil, Maldon and a screw of pepper, and lay them on whole fennel, equally treated, in a baking dish. Decorate with sprigs of fennel, and bake the little chaps for half an hour or so until their juices run clear. From the juices in the dish make a sauce by adding crème fraiche, a splash of white wine, and a dollop of fruit preserve of your choice. Peach and apricot are good. You might set them alight with brandy if the mood takes you.

They go well with pasta, and perhaps a dish of mushrooms.

Quail with Figs

Spreadeagle the birds and marinade for twenty-four hours in red wine, herbs and olive oil. Plunge them into hot oil to take colour and braise for a few minutes, having overlaid the breasts with bacon. Add white wine and a bunch of herbs, which should include sage, reduce the heat, and let them bubble happily away on top of the stove. When they're done (pierce with a skewer and see the juices run clear), remove, cut up the bacon and drape it decoratively over them. Add to the bubbling stock fig preserve and fresh figs in quarters. Toss the sauce over the ensemble.

The Failed Restaurateur

Before recounting our restaurant days, this is the moment to recall a salutary lesson. During the course of our travels, we also lived, for a year or so, in Bruges among the Flemish. We gazed from our apartment over the canals and treetops of the medieval city, the inner serenity meticulously preserved as though the millennia had melted away, and the city was scrubbed clean each morning. Bruges is the *Venice of the North*, and like *la*

Our apartment in Bruges (right), and the failed restaurant

Serenissima herself, entrances and seduces. When I think of music, said Nietzsche, I think only of the word Venice.

There are two drawbacks. First, sadly, one cannot help remarking, the locals themselves, whose grumpy endive features and odd shapes do nothing to enhance the visual splendour of their environment. They might easily be characterised as Bruegels, in recognition of the great Flemish master, rather than Brugels. As someone remarked, he had always thought Bruegel a superb caricaturist, populating his canvases with human gargoyles, grotesque cripples and the stumbling blind, until he saw the denizens of Bruges. Then he realised that Bruegel was a modest realist. There are no beggars in Belgium, only the surly, well-nourished bourgeoisie, who put up discouraging signs in their shops proclaiming, NO FREE ENTRY.

Despite this, Bruges is one of the most popular tourist destinations, perilously accessible to Europeans, particularly the English, always in desperate need of resuscitation. So the view from our windows, idyllic as it was, was debased by the chugs of tourist boats on the canals all day long, loudspeakers blaring commentaries in several languages. Streets are clogged. One seeks refuge in the restaurants.

Here, when it comes to food, Bruges and the Belgians excel (as they do with chocolate, the best in the world). Everything is hideously expensive, but the top quality shines, even drawing grudging respect from their French neighbours, who otherwise have jokes about them as the English do about the Irish. Simply to tell our French friends that we were moving to Belgium made them fall off their chairs with laughter. We ate in many wonderful establishments, but the one that stands out as a plaintive memoir was the one on the canal opposite our apartment.

We watched every day. Ravenous tourists stopped at the door. The position was unsurpassed, on the junction of two canals, and the restaurant looked attractive, cherry blossoms and lamplight casting Venetian reflections in the water at night. It was a romantic spot. The passers-by would study the menu on the door, peer through the window, and walk on. Once, a rowdy group of Spaniards seemed about to cross the threshold, but were drawn back by their moustachioed leader. Then, a party of six English scrubbers, baseball-capped and duckshit-shirted, ventured in. We held our breaths from our balcony far above. Five minutes later they emerged, and shuffled on.

Nobody ever stayed. One night we ventured down to check it out for ourselves. We peered through the window. A dim light flickered within. The tables were laid, starched linen, polished glasses, candelabra tall and unlit. It was pristine and sombre as a funeral. Then we picked out, silhouetted in the darkness, the profile of the patron. He wore a dinner jacket, black tie, and a worn pair of jeans. Cigarette in one hand, eyes glazed, he slumped on a chair, the condemned man having his last puff. We crept away.

Next morning, bright and early, we saw him arrive to open up, sure of another day of hopeless resignation. He held in his hands a bunch of leeks and a single punnet of strawberries. He was whistling as he closed the door carefully behind him.

Ratatouille

The important element is colour, so choose a vivid rainbow of vegetables, firm and fresh. Peppers red and yellow (avoid the green which taste like petrol), courgettes (always better young and skinny), onions (red if possible), mushrooms and aubergines. Ripe tomatoes.

This is a robust peasant vegetable stew so rough-cut the vegetables, each differently, for variety. Have the peppers in chunks, courgettes longways, mushrooms in half, onions and aubergines in rings, tomatoes whole. Nothing too thin. The only hint in preparation is to allow the aubergines to sweat under salt once you have sliced them.

Then the order of adding to the pot: in order of tenacity. Everything must amalgamate into a mix in which the ingredients still retain their individuality and stand out. It is a moment of balance, neither too sloppy nor over-assertive. So heat olive oil and add veg in order: first onions, allow to glaze but not brown; then aubergines which have sweated; then peppers, and the rest together with garlic and a clutch of fresh herbs so that the garlic does not burn. Add a screw of pepper, a dash of Maldon, splashes of oil as you go along and swizz around so that all fry lightly and take colour. Let them amalgamate and bubble. Toss in a glug of white wine with a cup of home-made chicken stock, never a cube. Turn the heat down, cover and cook slowly. Take off before they disappear into an indistinct mush.

Also very good added cold to pasta the next day or as a cold veg salad.

Running a Restaurant

Perhaps we should have had the poignant memory of the failed restaurant in Bruges in mind when we leapt into starting a restaurant ourselves. The great lesson on contemplating such a course is: *Don't!* Like the lure of having a second-hand bookshop, the myth of restaurants tempts and nourishes the fantasies of the romantic and the unwary. And never make the mistake of believing that just because you enjoy cooking for your friends you could manage a restaurant. There is no relation between the happy intimacy of exhibiting your culinary flair to a select handful, and taking on the anonymous masses. Running a restaurant is a nightmare, bedevilled with unpredictable and treacherous pitfalls. The public are not your friends.

The boma at our restaurant, set for lunch

We stumbled into it by default. After the years abroad, constantly on the move, we were weary with translating ourselves into many different languages and cultures, which is inevitably a process of dumbing down. We could order at a restaurant in French or Flemish, scour the markets for delectables, even entertain locals with limited conversation over dinner, but tell a joke or reach for depth, that we could not do. That is why invariably foreigners come across as superficial and humourless. They are not; it is the considerable barrier of language and its intricate cultural infusions that stumps one. In our case there was an edge of the comic to our forays into foreign languages. Linda could understand fairly well, but stumbled in speech. I could speak a bit but couldn't understand a word in reply. So you can imagine the clownish double act we presented: Linda translating as I launched into speech, struck dumb by each reply.

It was time to return to our roots, the comfort of familiarity. We were introduced to a property in the winelands by chance, and on an impulse bought it, taking along with us stoves and fridges, hopes and delusions. The landscape was reminiscent of the glories of Provence which we had left behind. If we narrowed our eyes we could almost hear the echoes of medieval knights thundering across the Vaucluse. Realistically, the town was neat and new, and by comparison bereft of illuminating food.

This is one of the steady complaints that I seek to illuminate. All over the world people take pride and care in cultivating and presenting foodstuffs of a ravishing variety. That is part of the thrill of travelling through country places and discovering the artistry and originality that abounds. It is an essential part of the culture of the country. Local people, often with no special training, throw themselves into making and growing food with as much gusto and discrimination as they consume it. There is everywhere a spirited, passionate, living culture of food, intimately bound to the society that nurtures it.

It is a lamentable and bewildering fact that there is hardly any trace of such enterprise in South Africa. Country towns are culinary deserts. It is the interminably duplicated and miserably uninteresting supermarkets that determine, and demolish, taste. Individuality and difference hardly exist. There is little sense of discrimination and consumer demands are marginal. Perhaps, after all, this is merely an accurate reflection of the broader cultural context.

Lamb Shanks

The bit of the leg that everyone salivates over is the shank. It is tender, succulent and sensual.

Take a fleshy shank per person, smear generously with Dijon mustard, and douse in balsamic vinegar. Lay them in a casserole dish splashed with olive oil, and throw over them splodges of chutney, a handful of garlic cloves, fresh rosemary, black pepper and Maldon.

Add a clump of whole vegetables to the pot: carrots, leeks, turnips, and put into the oven on high heat for half an hour. Then add red wine, turn the heat right down, and cook slowly for hours until the lamb is tender and juicy, falling off the bone. Remove the seared vegetables and rosemary, and serve the lamb with mashed potatoes or couscous, soaking up the juices. A sauce of yogurt spiced with chilli and lime juice sets it off.

Stuffed Lamb

Take a boned leg of lamb. Halve an aubergine and score each half with deep diamond cuts. Let olive oil soak into the cuts, and salt. Place the aubergine under the grill and toast thoroughly on both sides, adding more oil if required. Scoop out the grilled aubergine flesh from the skin and mash with garlic, a dozen anchovy fillets, a generous handful of diced olives, a shallot, lemon juice, rosemary, and a bit of diced chilli.

Open up the lamb, stuff with this mixture, and truss using skewers. Smear olive oil over the lamb, and roast in a medium oven. Use any extra stuffing as a bed for the lamb to repose on.

The Chef from Hell

We had hardly got started with our restaurant before the mad chef had one of his turns and stormed out of the kitchen, taking his motley crew with him. We were panic-stricken. Three days to the grand German dinner which Linda had secured as our first opportunity to put our new enterprise on the map. Neither of us had a clue how to prepare a dinner for a hundred guests so we scoured the town for casual helpers. We patched together a raggle-taggle bunch and dived into preparations. On the afternoon of the dinner the chef screeched back, hurled us and our makeshift crew out, and began throwing things together, himself in a panic, a couple of hours before the party arrived.

The instant he opened the cold room we knew we were sunk. The stench of rotten meat clouded out, almost knocking us off our feet at the far end of the restaurant. Gathering strength – for to confront the monster was always an epic affair – we told him flatly that we could not proceed with the meal. Our protestations were violently rejected. He was the chef and we knew nothing. The meat was simply well hung, so we could bugger off out of his kitchen.

The guests arrived, elegant in the garden which looked radiant by candlelight. Our stomachs in knots, we hovered over the serving of the first course, smoked salmon trout which could hardly go wrong. The sirloin was set upon the tables. The guests looked at their plates.

Nobody lifted a knife or fork. A murmur went up from every table: *Stinkendes Fleisch!*

We rushed to the kitchen to find the chef slumped next to his flagon of brandy. Now you explain, we pathetically urged. Tell them it's perfect, was what we got back.

The tour leader approached. We stammered and felt nauseous. Then, as the mutters were rising to a pitch, the chef, eyes blazing and lurching unsteadily, materialised on the veranda under the bright lights. Silence fell. The chef spoke: 'You fucking Krauts! Do you know how lucky you are to be here? How dare you return my food to the kitchen! Do you know who I am? Now fuck off back to where you came from!'

People sometimes speak of good restaurant experiences, but they never forget the terrible ones. They tell everyone they know, and they tell their friends. That we never had business from the tour operator again was predictable; the surprise was that we survived at all. Life shackled to the chef from hell had only just begun.

Thai Chubby

Cut tender chicken breasts, boned and skinless, into bite-size slivers. Season with lime or lemon juice, black pepper and Maldon. Peel and slice a good piece of ginger into long strips. Rinse or dust mushrooms, the wilder the better.

Into the pot, pour a can of coconut milk or cream. If concerned at the cholesterol rush, make up your own mixture with dried coconut and water or milk. Add the chicken, mushrooms and ginger, a dollop of brown sugar, a couple of spoons (depending on your heat resistance) of Thai curry paste – green, red or yellow – a few spoons of Thai fish sauce, a tin of drained water chestnuts, a handful of bamboo shoots, a few sprigs of lemon grass, some chopped coriander, and a few kaffir lime leaves from Thailand. Simmer until the chicken is tender. Don't overcook; it will toughen the chicken. It takes ten minutes or so. The aroma transports you immediately to the markets of Phuket.

The Thai curry paste is far preferable to the bottled sauces. When it comes to Thai ingredients, select those with the most incomprehensibly authentic labels.

Serve with Basmati rice and toss chopped coriander leaves on top.

Peanut Butter Chubby

Don't reveal the name of this dish to your guests since, lingering school sandwich prejudices apart, the peanut butter is the very last of the ingredients they will recognise.

Cut up the boneless and skinless chubby breasts, and marinade in soy sauce, ginger, several cloves of crushed garlic, and chilli to taste. Bake in the oven until tender, which will not take long.

For the sauce, to a pint of milk add a few dollops of peanut butter, more garlic, diced anchovy fillets, a squeeze of lemon, and a couple of spoons of brown sugar. Stir until it thickens and pour over chubby in its baking dish. Toss fresh coriander over the top.

You will delight and perplex your guests in the quiz to identify the ingredients. Some don't even get the chubby, and the peanut butter will be last. It is only once it is recognised that everyone exclaims, 'Yes, of course!'

Christmas Cheer

We had been open only a matter of weeks before Christmas struck. Fraught, frenetic weeks, leaving us frazzled. Shackled to the chef from hell, each hysterical trauma driving us towards destruction, we hung on. We had no alternative. The season was upon us and we needed to perform or go under. This was our only chance. After the season was over we would turn to tactics to resolve the situation. Him or us. If we survived that long.

Christmas morning, bright and blue. Restaurant buzzing with preparations: we were fully booked. Everyone chirpy despite working on Christmas Day. (Usual in the restaurant trade, and for double pay.) No sign of the chef.

He lurched in close to lunchtime, purple face blazing. Stormed the till and tore open the drawer. Everyone watching, astonished. Pulled out handfuls of notes and strode through the building throwing them in every direction.

'Help yourselves! These bastards' – gesticulating at Linda and me – 'won't give you anything. Happy Christmas!'

Staff diving after the fluttering notes. Linda and I struck with the horror of it.

Why didn't we react, scream, knock him down? It is never simple to deal with a monster. The staff were looking on. Customers would be arriving in half an hour. We didn't, anyway.

We had planned a buffet, and it was to provide a lesson we would never repeat. Quite ordinary people become transformed at the prospect of a buffet. They behave in ways they would never dream of with family or friends, or in their own homes. They become barbarians. The first ten people to reach the laden tables pile their plates until the food topples to the floor. They don't finish it, but abandon it halfway and stagger back for a second plate. Stuffed to the brim, this wasteful, shameful ritual goes on until the food has run out. Food for a hundred is squandered by ten gluttonous morons.

This is not much of an exaggeration. Deep-seated resentments must come to the surface at a buffet. Resentments which sink the restaurant, and generate pandemonium among the unfortunate customers who have held back.

Thus it was that the apoplectic old geezer who staggered across the lawn towards me might have had a point. Trouble was, he was pissed out of his mind on the half dozen gins he had put back, and his impatience at waiting for the buffet to be replenished had burst. He was out of his mind with fury and booze.

I saw him coming out of a corner of my eye. Restaurateurs develop a kind of twitching oscillation of head and neck as a trademark palsy. They are trying desperately to keep an eye on everything that is going wrong, and all those that might yet.

The old drunk gripped me around the throat with surprising, demented strength.

'I'm gonna kill you!'

Two hundred eyes stared at the spectacle, a hundred forks dangled in mid-air. I was lucidly aware that it would create a poor impression if I were to punch him in the head. I could see the newspaper headlines, 'OLD MAN ASSAULTED BY RESTAURANT THUG'.

So I prised his hands from my neck, emitting in a strangulated voice, 'I'm sorry, but I'm going to have to ask you to leave.'

Two hundred eyes returned to their groaning plates with a sense of relief. We never contemplated a buffet again. Christmas lunch would never be the same.

The Customer is not King

Nor is he always right, and it is absurd to carry on any business with that fixed assumption. It flies in the face of human nature. That you're in the service industry does not mean that you have to be on your hands and knees. You still have dignity, authority, rights, and indeed may well be right and the customer wrong. Like anyone else, and in any other context, the customer may simply be an arsehole.

I confess that when I reluctantly entered the restaurant business, my wary sense of human nature prepared me for the worst. I assumed I would be assailed by customers who were rude, violent, abusive and appallingly ugly. I imagined I would develop into a Basil Fawlty clone, lurching about in a state of hysteria and panic. I thought tenderly of the admirable John Fothergill, the rudest innkeeper in England and proprietor in the thirties of the legendary *The Spreadeagle* near Oxford, once the finest – and, according to Fothergill, the first – truly great restaurant in England. In order to cushion his sensitivities, Fothergill imagined compelling the really repellent customer to pay an entry fee, or wear a mask. I feared that most customers would prove offensive, but knew too, with a sinking heart, that I would not have the gall to enforce Fothergill's mask.

This was to be my major surprise. Much against my nature and preconceptions, almost all our customers were polite, appreciative and balanced. Not uncritical, but fair. Criticism, although very much suppressed in this country – where it is thought to be bad manners – is as essential an ingredient in keeping up standards in the restaurant business as it is in every other. Give up criticism and you will inevitably get the poor lot you deserve. Which translates in the restaurant world to indigestion, even food poisoning.

Compliments made it all seem, for a moment, worthwhile. Just as, quite disproportionately, one nasty customer could ruin not only the day, but sour one's sense of the business for days and weeks to come, ravaging one's sleep with unease.

I will be accused of terrible bias – perhaps bad taste – but I have to say that almost every objectionable customer who tried to make our lives a temporary misery was an English tourist. It pains me to record the fact, for in some ways I have always thought of myself, or a part of me, as English, my dad never having relinquished his Yorkshire blood. There is something peculiarly repellent about some Englishmen on holiday. The majority of course are as sweet and kind as anyone else, if that is the way you see human nature, but the exceptions are from Brixton, Birmingham and Brighton, not Boston, Beijing or Bordeaux. If your sheltered upbringing or ironclad political correctness still make you shun this stunningly obvious truth, think of the football hooligan. In what language do you shudder?

Perhaps the situation is exacerbated in this country in virtue of our Colonial past. This impels the odd touring Englishman to assume his God-given right to treat us as servants, the worse the better. Of course in entering a restaurant he is encouraged to give full vent to this instinct. What are we there for if not to serve and tremble? We could with time see this kind of Little Englander approaching. There is something in the walk, something in the hideousness of dress, something in the flush of face. He marches in and the volume of talk is shattering. He takes over, he has arrived. He flicks his fingers, even whistles, at the waiters. He throws himself into a chair and gets rapidly pissed.

One late lunchtime I was called to a table by a frustrated waitress who could not cope any further. She filled me in. The table – indeed, English tourists – had ordered meanly and scrimpingly, and were at the end of the meal vociferously complaining and refusing to pay the bill. It is invariably the case with this sort that the order is as lean and parsimonious as it is possible to be in a restaurant without actually passing out from starvation. The insult is in the huge disparity in value between this country and theirs, worsened of course by the mighty pound in relation to the miserable rand. The price of our restaurant meal would be a tenth of what they would expect to pay at home. Here the money goes on the booze.

So there they were, pissed as farts, belligerent and loud. Their spokesman fixed me with a red and watery eye. I've put in italics what I would have liked to respond; alas, my real responses were as prosaic as they were compelled to be.

'Look 'ere mate,' gesturing to the empty plate on the table.

I'm not your mate, you ugly little rodent.

'This leaf,' pointing at the last chewed bit of lettuce on the plate.

I'd like to ram it down your throat.

'Worms.'

Worms to you, mate.

'It were worms what did it.'

Nothing like what I'd like to do to you.

Then, with a flourish, he gestured to the empty plates of the other three in his party, which were shining as though licked clean. He fixed me with a conspiratorial eye.

' 'Ow does I know they 'aven't ate theirs? Worms, mate, worms.'

As I stared dumbfounded, he reached the point of the drama. He folded his arms across his chest, slit his eyes.

'We ain't paying.'

In the early days I'd have forced the issue, insisted they cough up, called the police. It's not worth it, or not to me. I remembered the drunk woman who threw her plate at the wall when asked to settle the bill, the drunk driver who rammed his new BMW into the gate in apoplexy. I lapsed into a karmic daze over the years, feeling less stressed by accommodating and compromising – letting it go – however much the customer was in the wrong.

So I said, 'All right. I'll take your salad off the bill. But the others stay.'

He looked unhappy.

'That your best offer?'

Please go away and don't come back.

'We won't be back.'
Ah!
I tell you, you can't win.

Chefs

We seemed particularly hard done by with the chef we had, but there is perhaps rarely any approaching a congenial one. Chefs are frustrated actors, most often ham actors, and sometimes clowns. As any circus child knows, not all clowns are funny, or good. There is always the nasty one who lights the firecrackers under the other's bottom, and gets away with it.

As our nightmare chef would often scream, 'Showtime, darling!', throwing his arms wide and pirouetting in his billowing kaftan.

We were thrust – should have been kicking and screamimg – into bed (so to speak) with our chef, but most times one has some choice. Exercise it judiciously. A rigorous interview and checking of references is essential. When it comes to chefs, believe nothing. Go through the process exhaustively, talk openly to anyone who has worked with them, dig and delve while you have the chance, for it will soon be too late. The chef is the centre of the enterprise, and there is nothing that will ruin it more quickly than the wrong one. The most vital clause in your contract with a chef is how to fire him quickly and with minimum pain and disruption. Since you may well wish to do this in mid-season, even mid-dinner, it is not always practicable, something the chef knows well. Thus he tends to crack 'under pressure' just when you need him most. Best solution is to have another on standby, but that is rarely achievable.

The chef has the restaurant at his mercy, and he knows it. If he is the wrong one, it feels like blackmail. Even if he is right, his sense of power and ego may prove overwhelming. The restaurant, he believes, *is* himself. Why else would people come? This works, if precariously, while he is fashionable and the restaurant successful, although the owners, managers, staff – even the poor deluded customers – are ever at his mercy. He throws a tantrum – and this is the norm – and the meal is ruined, the restaurant in tatters.

It is something of a mystery how the chef has taken on the mantle of celebrity. It is much the same with fashion models. Not long back, the chef was a cook, and like any other tradesman he laboured away, and his place in the great scheme of things was modest. Just as models were airheads who had failed at typing school. Now we have Claudia and Naomi, Marco Pierre and Jamie. Television has exacerbated the process of inflation to unbearable levels. It does not now appear possible to cook unless you do it on the box. It is sheer narcissism. Nigella confounds in eclipsing the categories, and inventing herself as a model chef. The way to a man's stomach is through the TV screen.

It were not ever thus. The spawning of the Frankenstein celeb chef is part of the general move to television idolatry. Chef icons have always lurked in the background, casting impressively dark and discreet shadows. Brillat-Savarin, Escoffier, Michel Roux ... so remote that they attained the mystique of gods. Only in conformity to the pop media culture of the age have the eminences descended from Olympus to prance and posture for the masses (their fans). Sometimes the cooking skills appear to take second (or tenth) place to other more shining television attributes: youthfulness, sex appeal, mateyness, puckered charm. This is all well and good, but it is a far cry from the essence of the matter: the ability to cook.

It is unfortunately not only the chefs who are unaware of how absurd their antics are. The guzzling, ogling public is gullible, and often encourages the excesses. It's theatre after all! Chefs make the mistake of taking themselves with bloody-minded seriousness, but there should be no reason for us to put up with it. It is an arena for prima donnas, and attracts a disproportionate number of gays (too many), and of women (too few). My personal worst are the pig-faced strutting little prima donnas, short men with huge egos, who shave their heads and wear a ring through their ear. It is as disconcerting a look as waiters with rings through their tongues.

The trade also attracts the deadbeats, no-hopers who have tried everything else, confidence tricksters and poseurs. Once they have reached the end of the road – even the estate agent cap has fallen off – they pass themselves off as chefs. In my experience of restaurant ownership, a somewhat *film noir* example of the wrong chef stands out, so curdling that it could only have been desperation that drove us to take him on. It was.

We were caught in mid-season with chefs flouncing out (chefs don't walk), and crises of numbers that made it imperative that we find replacements immediately. So we were rash, but under extreme duress. Perhaps only those who have been at the forefront of the restaurant business can understand the sense of desperation that overwhelms one as another two hundred customers march through the doors, and there is nobody to cook for them. The immediacy is compelling. You are ready to embrace the next man in an apron and funny hat.

He appeared a fit and keen young man with a list of impressive places he had worked at. He did not wear a funny hat and looked fresh and robust. He threw himself into production in the midst of chaos and came up smiling. He saved us, and was so charming and energetic that we were remiss in not checking out his past too carefully. He glibly sweet-talked us when one restaurant had no memory of him. ('Change of ownership. Guy's in Namibia now. Good friend. I'll get him to call.') He ducked and dived when another was ambiguous. ('Had a fallout with the head chef. Nasty queen. Did me some damage.') By the time we realised something was terribly wrong, we were shackled to him.

The revelation arrived in the form of a letter which asked if we were aware that our chef had tried to kill his father, and had been in prison for attempted murder.

We were thrown into crisis. We realised that all his references were lies, and that his cooking skills had been acquired in the prison kitchen. Yet we had come to like him, and he coped with the summer hordes with enviable energy. He seemed tame as one of the hundreds of lambs he turned expertly on the spit. And yet ... I could not help eyeing the long kitchen knives with foreboding.

He stayed for some time, long enough to get us through that season anyway, and give us time to find a less homicidal replacement. His sojourn was not without drama. One afternoon he rushed to me wild-eyed and asked to hide in the office. I had just given him the message that someone called Juan had called from Betty's Bay.

'He's here!' blurted the chef as he hurled himself behind some crates in the office and locked himself in.

Juan had evidently not phoned from Betty's Bay. He must have been two minutes away, and wanted to ascertain that the chef was there. The moment he arrived my sympathies were with the chef. A black Mustang with blacked out windows roared into the parking lot, screeched to a stop in a swirl of dust. On the bonnet of the car was emblazoned in silver the word *BANDIT*.

The driver's door flung open and out stepped a midget dressed in black from head to toes, which were encased in pointed black boots. What caught my eye was the disproportionate size of the gun that bulged from the minuscule bandit's belt. He looked like Clint Eastwood from the Seven Dwarfs. His short legs got him to me faster than I could imagine, and I was able to maintain a straight face in telling him the chef he was after had only moments before fled without warning in the direction of the river. The bandit pulled away in hot pursuit.

Not that the chef was grateful. A week later, I was surprised to get a couple of calls from town making offers on our fridges and stoves.

'Oh yes,' they assured me, 'the chef offered them to us at a very reasonable price.'

I suspect the bastard stole my gold wristwatch, a legacy of my father's, and on that ground alone it was a blessing to get rid of him. No doubt he is suavely gulling his way through the restaurants of the west coast. Using us as a reference, of course.

Tamarind Curry Chubby

Slice skinless and boneless chubby breasts with the grain. Douse in lemon juice. Infuse a gobbet of sticky tamarind paste with some dried peaches in hot water.

Into a hot pan, toss butter and curry powder (in this case, koknie masala). Remember that curry needs a rush of intense heat to bring it to life. When you feel the heat in your nostrils, throw in the chubby pieces. Let them sear and take on the burnt umber tincture of the curry.

Add the softened peaches, a handful of diced coriander, slices of ginger, a few smashed cloves of garlic, and a couple of bay leaves. Toss the ingredients about, and when they look ready, add the tamarind infusion (which will be peach tinted). Let it bubble away until you are overcome with the heady spicy aroma, and the chicken is cooked.

Chubby la Veuve

In her mountain fastness above the Keurbooms River, the noble Widow seeks solace – and delights her guests – with superb dinners, candelabras flickering in the farmhouse kitchen,

Sylvester fluttering attendance, and protected by rhinos, Louis the mastiff, and myriad butterflies. She tosses it all together with a nonchalance and flair that are signs of instinctive taste. She has the eye, as well as the palate.

This spontaneous dish, which has her minions drooling at her feet, the Widow insists should be made with 'nice plump little bastards' (referring to the chickens of course). Attack them with these condiments in a ratio that appeals to your palate:

tomato sauce
soy sauce
honey
lemon juice
Worcester sauce
chutney
sweet chilli sauce

Massage it all in, grinding black pepper and Maldon over the top and scattering fresh rosemary and hunks of onion and green pepper. Douse with olive oil. Then thrust into a hot oven to sear for fifteen minutes, turning the chubby until brown and singed. Turn the heat down low, and slowly bake for a couple of hours until tender and falling apart in the juices.

Cut it up, and immerse in the juices. Do not be put off by the quantity of juice, it sets the palate a-tingle. Chubby is crispy on the outside and delectably succulent within. The Widow serves all her dishes lukewarm.

Doing it in Public

Look around the restaurant.

Poor postures, bodies slumped forward on uncomfortable chairs, dressed like people in post office queues. The lights make their faces like corpses. A fork dangles in mid-air, waves about, it's too full. Stabs at the mouth, you can see inside. Jaws churn, chins wobble, some green bits slide out of the corner of the mouth. Splodges are stuck to teeth. Some have a glazed, bored look and are silent and sulky. They are the married couples. Others talk with mouths full of masticated bits. You notice a buttock discreetly lifted from the seat. You want to go home.

What induces us to make exhibitions of ourselves eating in public? It is not an attractive exercise. However scrupulous we are, self-conscious to the point of hardly being able to enjoy the experience at all, eating is a curiously unappetising affair, as far as other people are concerned. Remember how warily we scrutinised our lovers on those early dates? How easily we were put off by the way someone chewed, or ran the tongue over the teeth. How careful we were at where we aimed the fork, how much dangled from it, swallowing before we spoke, suppressing burps and farts. And still desperately trying to be romantic and sexy.

Draw a curtain round each table, avert the gaze. This is in the interests not so much of a natural modesty – that we have clearly lost – but of self-preservation. We need to save ourselves from having to look at others stuffing their faces.

A worthy inheritor to the great John Fothergill, who, you'll recall, wanted repugnant customers to wear a mask, was the notorious Tickell, to whose pub outside Cambridge (*The Tickle Arms*) I made many pilgrimages, partly for the place and the food, but primarily for the host. It was not a pub as such, and certainly there was none other of its kind. First, there was no sign or indication that it was a public house at all. Tickell would nail his rules to the front door, which were an expression of his prejudices of the week. *No Men With Beards. No Long-Haired Lefties. No Women in Trousers.* His head, adorned in a nightcap with a bell attached, would pop blearily out of the window above the door. When he emerged, sheathed in a velvet dressing gown, he was irascible and taciturn. He carried a soda siphon, and attacked with founts of spray anyone who had the temerity to smoke. Yet people loved it, even the drenched ones, and flocked to be abused, or amused, by the most eccentric innkeeper in the world. The food, by the way, was exceptionally fine, and the house a work of fastidious taste. But it would all have been for nothing without the curmudgeon who gave it personality and style.

It remains safer, and saner, to keep eating a private affair. There is no need to subject ourselves to the scrutiny of random strangers, or have to watch them with rising nausea. We do not perform our ablutions in public, we are shy of bodily functions. Yet we unembarrassedly reveal the intricacies of mastication and ingestion to strangers who are probably looking at us with as much horror as they provoke in us. We are not Romans sitting happily round the baths together, letting it all hang out, nor are we dashing to the vomitorium between courses.

If we share the experience of eating, it should be with friends and lovers. As with sex, promiscuity palls, or appals, and we learn to discriminate and reserve our tastes. Promiscuous eating habits bring on indigestion. Friends and lovers we can digest, and the experience of eating together takes on a different quality. It gels with the forms of intimacy, exposure, and familiarity – even tolerance – that we share. We are comfortable, and can afford a level of indulgence. Food, in this context, becomes an integral part of the experience, enhancing and enriching. We can stomach it.

The Party from Hell

Whenever there is a restaurant party, there is a tacit competition, sometimes breaking into open warfare, rather like a beauty pageant. Perhaps it is human nature to eye what everyone else has, and make sure you haven't lost out. There is inevitably a winner, and runners-up doing deals.

This is the sort of scene I eavesdropped on many times in my career as restaurateur.

'Could I taste yours? Just a mouthful ...'

'I can swap a bit of duck for a prawn ...'

'Don't be so mean, I only want to dunk the bread in your sauce ...'

'Just *look* at what John's got. Damn it, he's always right!'

Many women infuriate their men by simply leaning over and grabbing from the plate, often taking the moral high ground to conceal their greed, 'You know it's not good for your cholesterol ...'

It is inevitable, too, that nothing is quite as good as it looked, or as someone else has chosen, or as it was last time.

There is always someone at the table who ruins the party. You are all settling in, the restaurant looks great, there is a happy buzz. Then the food arrives.

Someone looks at his plate askance. Beckons to the waiter.

'Excuse me, this steak is too rare. I said medium rare ...'

Or he might say, 'This is not right. If you look at the menu, it says ...'

His face is crumpled with irritation. The waiter whisks the plate away. Now everyone else has to wait. You're starving. The whole meal is put on hold as the problem is rectified.

What actually happens in the kitchen is never admitted by the restaurant, and of course no such thing ever happened in ours. A returned plate disrupts the flow, and irritates the chef. He simply takes the returned plate, spits on it, rubs it round the toilet seat, and returns it to the customer. A sous-chef is scrabbling in the bin picking bits of chewed chicken legs to add to another complaining customer's casserole. Your order sits sweltering under the warmer, congealing and suppurating.

The food finally arrives. The waiter slams down the plates. Nobody is happy, but they are sensible enough not to complain. The wait has been onerous. The guest from hell is at it again.

'Now look at it. Overdone, of course. I tell you, I won't be coming back here.'

Someone is apologising to the harassed waiter, 'Don't worry, he's a miserable bastard.'

You pretend not to take notice, and he chomps away with a grim expression. No wonder. It tastes like shit. Everyone else is infected with the sense of dissatisfaction. Conversation falters. It is unmitigated selfishness.

There is a level of ponciness that some people adopt when they go to a restaurant. They put on airs, and behave in a way they would never dream of doing at home, where they eat overcooked steak, never daring to complain, and drink wine out of a box. In the restaurant they are world experts in every nuance of finesse, and are never satisfied. They sniff the wine, roll it around their tongues, and say it's not the 96 vintage they prefer. They say the calamari is not as crisp as it was last time, or the salad dressing could do with a touch of sugar.

'Excuse me, you might be interested, I'm only saying this for your own good, if you add a little more lemon to your tartare to balance the cucumber it will taste better.'

It's not worth it. Enter a restaurant in a spirit of largesse and a lack of pettiness, or stay miserably at home. If you don't like it, no one will force you to go back. At least you won't have ruined the occasion for everybody else.

Just the Bill

Imagine you are a woman alone at a restaurant. There is a man alone at a table on the far side of the room. He pulsates sensuality. Your eyes meet. There is unbelievable chemistry. A throbbing expectation mounts. Then you watch as he calls for the bill.

He takes out his glasses, scrutinises it for some time. Too long. Purses his lips. His mouth suddenly looks different. He summons the waiter. Stabs at the bill with a finger. That, too, now looks stunted. His voice rises in semi-quavers.

'There was one glass of wine, not two. And it was the shiraz, not the merlot. There's a difference, right? Yes, but that's included in the special. No, I won't pay extra for the rice, I don't like the potato fritter. You wanna call the manager? All right then, subtract the wine from the cognac, and I'll pay the difference. Not a cent more.'

He wrangles and saves a buck or two, but he's lost you for ever. The fantasy has been squirted with a fire extinguisher.

The crunch comes in every meal when the bill arrives. Blossoming romances wilt, wives raise tired eyes to the ceiling, someone makes a feeble grasp in the direction of the bill and misses, someone else has always just left the table with convenient bladder syndrome. There is always an asshole who takes charge. He snatches it up with an imperious look at the waiter, as if he is the host. He doesn't reach for his pocket, but addresses the table. His eyes are scouring the bill like lasers.

'So this is the damage, folks. Mervyn, you had the scallops I think, and Dora yours was the carpaccio. Shit, they don't come cheap! Sylvia, you had dessert, right. And the extra cappuccino was yours, Virgil. Moira and I had chicken, you had a half portion didn't you, doll? I didn't have a starter, so let's subtract ...'

He takes out a calculator.

'Two bottles of wine. But then I don't drink, so the Coke's mine, but we must divide this by five not six, am I right? Oh, you only had half a glass, lovey ...?'

And he smiles. And these are his friends. His wife is still with him.

Nobody stabs him with a fork, nobody throws up. He even pays with his card (gold, of course), collecting cash from the others, not bothering with details of change. He scoops up the bill to submit to his accountant and says, 'For the taxman.'

As a parting shot, 'Look after the tip would you, Merv. I'm outta change.'

How many beautiful friendships have not shuddered to a standstill on such nights, how many hearts have not stopped. There is nothing like a restaurant bill to bring out true natures. It is not a matter of money, it never is. It's everything else. Be prepared to abandon friends and lovers, and despair.

Ouma Lien's Malva

Every ouma has a malva in her somewhere. This is the best. It should be, as it comes from my nephew Ollie's ouma, and he is a fussy little fellow. I'll never forget the tantrum he threw at a restaurant – *my* restaurant! – when there was no cranberry jelly on the table. He was five. Get it right for Ollie.

Beat two eggs with a large cup of sugar and add a tablespoon of apricot jam. Melt a blob of butter with a teaspoon of vinegar, and add to the beaten egg mix, together with a wine glass of milk.

Sift a large cup of flour (same amount as the sugar) with a teaspoon each of bicarb and vinegar, and fold into the wet ingredients. Bake in a pie dish at medium heat for about forty-five minutes. Test for readiness with a fork that should come out clean.

The sauce, which is thrown over the cooked malva hot from the oven, is composed of a cup of water, a small tin of unsweetened evaporated milk, a quarter of a butter block, a scant cup of sugar, brought to the boil.

The pudding is golden, treacly, and irresistible, served tepid with lashings of custard.

Peach Whip

This is a straightforward, fresh and light pudding, but I will endeavour to make it sound as salacious as possible, so as not to bore you with simplicity. Peach whip, indeed.

Mash half a dozen sweet ripe peaches, from which you have stripped the silken skin. It is more delectable to do this with a fork and finish it off with your fingers, than resort to the dreary old blender. Lick the pulp from your fingers, and savour the juices. There is no fruit sexier than a peach, redolent of blushing bottoms and succulent flesh, so linger over picking the peachiest before you begin. Test for perfection with subtle pinches to the flesh, and caresses to the skin.

Beat two egg whites stiffly, and add a bare espresso cup or eggcup of castor sugar. Beat again, and put in as much sugar again. Drip in the peach pulp, and beat again until it is airy and fluffy. As your wrist begins to weaken with all this unaccustomed exercise, take fortitude in reminding yourself of the wisdom of our rustic forefathers, ghastly old perverts that they were:

A woman, a dog, and a walnut tree:

The more you beat them, the better they be.

The whip – now you see why – is chilled in the fridge and topped with whipped (it's not over yet, I'm afraid) cream. Decorate with sprigs of mint, glacé cherries, and the imprint of a kiss from the lover who drove you to it.

Meringues with Strawberries

Strawberries go particularly well with meringues, but it could equally be peaches, raspberries or Cape gooseberries. Every fruit, as D H Lawrence observed, has its secrets.

Combine a teaspoon each of vanilla essence, vinegar and water. Whip three egg whites until stiff, together with half a teaspoon of baking powder and a pinch of salt. Add spoons of sifted sugar (you will need a cup in all) alternately with spoons of the combined liquid. Continue to beat for some time until you have a fairy castle rising before your eyes.

Scoop the castle on to a baking plate, hollow out the centre and build the battlements, turrets and cupolas that appeal to you. Bake in a very low oven for an hour or more until the outside is crisp and the inside still sticky. Let the meringue cool and smother it with strawberries that have soaked in white wine, castor sugar and black pepper. Screw more black pepper over the strawberries with whipped cream.

The Ideal Restaurant

What is it that makes one restaurant succeed and another fail? What is it that spurs one to choose this restaurant above another? What are the ingredients of the ideal restaurant?

It is not the food. Or not exclusively, even primarily, so. This truth, which might appear hard to swallow, is readily demonstrable. Imagine the meal of your dreams. But the restaurant is dingy, the service atrocious, the patrons ugly; the place is redolent of old farts.

Then conjure up the restaurant of your dreams, albeit the food indifferent, such that you hardly recall what you ate. Tasteful (your taste), radiant waitresses, surrounded by the beautiful and fragrant. There is something about it, which you can't quite put your finger on ... It even works in the homely trattoria where everything is authentic, unpretentious and convivial.

Of course, the food cannot be vile. This suggests that there is a sliding scale, a matter of relativity, in the subtle mix that makes up the ideal restaurant. The ideal restaurant has to be experienced as that; it means nothing as a shrine on its own. Thus it is not a matter of getting it right on paper, or in theory, but of putting the right idea into practice. The test of a restaurant is in the way it works.

Here we confront what I call the German Fallacy.

However diligent the good Germans may be at putting together a car or transistor, they are beside themselves that they cannot do it with food or wine (and, for all I know, with sex). They laboriously imitate every last detail of French production and style, and their version lacks the very ingredient that makes the French magic. At the very moment of triumph – and it took Friedrich Nietzsche, as a German, to recognise it – the cry of horror! This is the secret that the cunning French have a phrase for: *je ne sais quoi*. That which is not known, but its presence is essential to the result. It is a mystery that cannot be translated. It's in the very air that is breathed, the very nostrils and palates, the fingers and toes, the blood, the *terroir* and the tradition. It is something endemic, evanescent, indefinable – but without it the wine tastes of sugar and the food of sausage.

If we apply this argument to our sense of general knowledge, we distinguish between things that we know in the head, as theory, and those we need to know *for ourselves*. The first category is knowing what things are, in the way that we know the moon, Einstein's theory of relativity, Saddam Hussein and Hitler. This is what the Germans know of French methodology in food and wine, the textbook version. In fact, most things that we know are of this kind, the frail facts that sustain us. We know but we don't know. We have a derivative, secondhand understanding – we've read about it – but we may well be surprised at how flimsy our grasp, how disappointing the result, when we put it to the test.

It is quite different with things we need to experience directly to know them at all. Things we are unable to know unless we know what they're *like*, how they feel, or taste. Here we enter the labyrinth of emotions, psychology and intuitions: the dark realm of what lies under the surfaces. We do not know what love is, or jealousy, or sexual climax, until or unless we have experienced them for ourselves. We almost have to *become* these things to know them, from the inside as it were. It is the same with food.

Knowing food relies on having a taste for it and having tasted it for ourselves. We know what we like because we have experienced the tastes for ourselves. It is no good being told about it, we need to do it directly. Food permeates below the surface of ordinary facts, and reaches into the labyrinth of desires and primal senses. We ingest certain kinds of knowledge like food.

This process makes each of us what we are. It makes up the inner workings of our subjective selves, our tastes and desires. We know such things with an immediacy and directness that seem transparent, even if they are often difficult to explain or put into words. This is what makes the language of lovers, as much as that of lovers of food, seem so clichéd. We simply cannot find words original and adequate enough to match the sensations we have been through. To describe or write enlighteningly about sex or food are challenges not for the fainthearted. For most people, a sigh, grunt, or susurration of contentment are as much as they can manage.

But it is not enough. The lover really wants more than that from the loved one, wants to know how it really feels, what it really means. Meaning, and meaningfulness, is more than a sigh or a burp, however satisfied. So we all, lovers of each other, of food, or whatever else takes our fancy, need to articulate a language that puts across the way we really feel. Without that, we are trapped in the happy little world of our subjective satisfactions, and we can never go further. The solitary glutton is as miserable as the lonely masturbator.

Let us apply this thoughtful little canter to our quest for the perfect restaurant. The ingredients we are looking for are drawn from this realm of subjective emotion, psychology and intuition; in other words, from our own underworld of tastes, habits and assumptions. The quest for the ideal meal, the restaurant of our dreams, is akin to the quest for the ideal lover. We need to recognise, and savour them for ourselves. We digest our lovers like meals, our meals like lovers. We know when it is perfect. But it might not be the same for someone else.

This suggests that the ideal restaurant is not a thing in itself, but is only what each different patron might experience it as. In a sense it is a figment of the imagination. The perfect restaurant, like the lover, is what we experience as the perfect restaurant, and it is different for everybody. This would be a difficult conclusion for restaurateurs to accept. How could they possibly begin, for they might only attract one customer? The ideal restaurant is one perfectly *for you*.

It is never a matter exclusively of the food. Where we are, who we're with, the complete context, makes up the total experience. Why does food invariably taste better in a foreign country (well, most), or with the perfect companion? And always best when we're really hungry. We do not arrive innocent at the experience of food. Even in our appetite and expectations lurk our histories. We take ourselves along with us, and that is not always to our benefit or enlightenment. We need to pretend, at least, that we are open to the new and surprising, that we are more innocent than we are. *Rasa* the *tabula* as you enter the restaurant of your dreams.

The Ideal Restaurant, part 2

There is no such thing as the ideal restaurant, as if it were cast in stone, or sung in heaven. Just as there is no ideal book or picture or lover. It all depends on the person who is judging, and we are all rather different, which is to our great fortune. There is no more depressing thought than to imagine us all the same. We are, after all, individuals, or we try to be. We bring along our own perspectives, values, and experience to any situation, and we choose, evaluate and act accordingly. This is what makes us go in one direction rather than another, be with someone rather than someone else, eat this rather than that, or in this restaurant, not the one across the road.

But just because there is no ideal, no absolute best (or at least none we could all agree on), does not mean that everything is the same either, or that we cannot tell good from bad, and many shades along the way. Of course we can; we do it all the time. There is an appalling (and dishonest) pressure on people to step back from making distinctions and discriminations, as if it were bad form, or they were caught with their pants down. They do not want to be landed with anything as risky as a judgement, and are almost embarrassed by an opinion. Who am I to judge? is their pathetic cry. (I'm not being judgemental, they say, as if it were a virtue.) This is arrant nonsense. It comes through a fuzzy, politically correct climate of shilly-shallying, spin doctoring, non-committal, and glib relativism. It has something to do with a loss, or abandonment, of standards, yardsticks, and critical faculty, what we ordinarily call thinking. We are certainly the poorer for it, and feel its absence acutely in the kitchen, the restaurant, and the bedroom.

We have mental lists of what we like, approve of, and how much. We have a pretty good picture in our own minds of how things add up for us. Without such a storehouse we could hardly operate coherently. We would reel from one meal to another, stagger from one restaurant to another, pitch from one lover to the next, without rhyme or reason. In fact, we have our minds made up, and we act within a rather narrow orbit of pleasures and choices. We know, more or less, what we like. It is hardly surprising, then, that our ingredients are pretty general, and look something like everyone else's.

When it comes to restaurants, we look to our storehouse, and pull out the ingredients that make sense in this context. We put ourselves forward, and reveal aspects of our ways of appreciating and selecting, not simply in restaurants. Our tastes come into play, our aesthetic sense, our sense of space and place. We choose and judge restaurants on the food, certainly, but the food in relation to other important elements that make up the total restaurant experience. It can even happen that everything else is so *simpatico*, that we forgive the ordinariness of the food.

We can list the elements in a general way, and in the end it boils down to something we call ambience, which is rather difficult to pin down. It would be made up of some elements of decor and lighting, comfort, relaxation and warmth, the attitude and attractiveness of the service, originality of ingredients, the *style* of the place, the *feeling* we get. Each element is weighted according to our particular sense of relative importance. There is often a sense of surprise, pleasant or stimulating.

Perhaps it is all theatre. Indeed, the theatrical element is strong in a restaurant, and we are part of the show. There is a complicity, a contract between role players. We are there to act (or show off), and they put on an act for us. Here, I think, we have it. The most important element in a restaurant is magic, or fantasy. We enter a world different from that of our own home and kitchen and friends, the elements that make up our everyday eating experiences. We are transported, and that is the sensation we seek. We take ourselves there, but it is up to the restaurant to take us somewhere else. That somewhere is the expression of our fantasies (as far as this experience goes), and the restaurant plays a conjuring trick which panders to our dreams. Restaurants are brothels with desirable whores, good enough to eat.

Freshers Veal

This original dish is named in honour of its originator, my great friend Peter, and I hasten to record it for posterity, as the last time he tried to remember it Barbara added mushrooms and wine, much to our consternation.

Season veal escalopes with Maldon, black pepper and lemon juice. Beat them with a mallet to ensure tenderness. Sizzle over the stove with olive oil, a smidgen of garlic, a sliver of mace, and two whole star anise. Remove the veal, which takes a couple of minutes to cook so it is succulent and pink, and keep warm.

To the juices add a generous scoop of Chinese Five Spice powder, and flambé with the best brandy you can lay your hands on. It is worth turning off the lights for the vivid effect of the leaping blue flames, particularly thrilling for gawking children. Let the flames die down, simmer momentarily and throw in dollops of crème fraiche or thick cream, together with – the true genius of the dish – a handful of freshly grated parmesan cheese. (Avoid the pre-grated variety in small packets which tastes of vomit.) Mix it up to a thick silky sauce to dowse the veal.

Incomparably relished at Freshers in the summer rose garden.

Mr K's Café

Mr K (as I call him) turned the bait shop on the corner into a trendy restaurant. To show how trendy it was he called it a café. This is not original, of course (it is long a token of blasé chic in London), but when I mooted it years ago for our restaurant, the partner thought it would be confused with what we used to call the Greek shop on the corner.

What Mr K did might stand for more or less an ideal kind of restaurant. It is not smart, and does not aspire to

Peter and Linda (and crayfish) in the kitchen at Freshers

be chic, although people who go there often are. They dumb down for the seaside, and feel dangerously excited by the salt tang in the air, the constipated cry of gulls, the drunks rolling on the pavement. But – and here is the acid test – it works.

It has style, ambience, feeling. Even soul. A sign slapped to the kitchen wall says, *Fire your boss today*. The waiters are sassy, but they're efficient and calm, and they know the regulars. You sit down and your cappuccino and glass of water arrive. That makes you feel wanted. Yet the waiters rule, and that's how it should be. They know their business, as do the chefs. They yell and pirouette before everyone's eyes, but they know exactly what they're doing. You watch a cool ballet. The food is fresh, original, and chalked on a blackboard.

The sense of fisherman's café persists. Walls are crumbling and paint smeared. Tables bare and mismatched. An eclectic mix of paintings hung for sale, irises in milk bottles, postcards sent by customers as they travel (often risqué), bunches of roses. It hangs together. People traipse in and out carrying fish and meat and vegetables. You stumble across them on the way to the loo. Bundles of notes cross the counter. Everything happens in front of you. It is casual and looks spontaneous, but there is an eye that oversees all, and it's right. Music plays, funky but not too loud. It is vital to get music right in any restaurant. Nothing worse than background elevator music, nor acid rock. People here come not only to eat or grab a croissant. They come to talk, tap at their pc's, play chess, listen to Kenneth's zany laugh. The locals gather, and many a lazy afternoon has been whiled away here in jolly company, best with Alain (the Councillor) and Elaine (Lady Russell), stalwarts of Kalk Bay, and steadfast friends.

One drawback: no reservations. So one has to choose an offbeat moment, and never on Sunday mornings, when the trippers in their BMs swarm in from up the line. Now can I have that table permanently on hold, Mr K?

Lamb Couscous with Harissa

Soak a cup of chickpeas in water overnight.

Into the pot: tender diced lamb – brown in olive oil with a screw of pepper, Maldon and lime zest. Add the chickpeas, a couple of sliced carrots, sliced red onion and turnip, stick of cinnamon and six of the best cardamom seeds whole. Let them all take colour, add water to cover, and simmer. The kitchen is filled with the most delicious aroma.

When the lamb is nearly done, toss in some mangetout, strips of leek and whole baby tomatoes. Let the ingredients retain their individual identities. There should be generous liquid to cook and then slush over the couscous.

For the harissa: slice some peppers of different colours, removing seeds, and blacken under the grill to sear the skins. Peel the peppers, tear into strips, and pulverise with olive oil, juice of two limes, hot chilli and garlic to taste. The mix will be the colour of golden desert sand and should retain some chunkiness. It should taste just too hot: remember you are to eat it with a dish that is not in itself hot.

Couscous is the simplest and most beguiling dish to make. It sounds exotic but takes one minute to prepare. Simply add liquid from the pot to cover the couscous (one cup between two people), bring to the boil for an instant and remove. The fine grains absorb the liquid immediately. Separate and fluff up.

Present the couscous in a pretty bowl, and the pot of lamb sprinkled with fresh coriander. Serve the dish of harissa separately.

Fraserburg Lamb

This is one of several lamb dishes which rely on long, slow cooking. This one was put in a *bakoond* at a civilised time in the morning, and consumed late in the afternoon by a dozen pleasantly inebriated guests on the stoep at Lawrence and Sarah's *Boomhuis* in Fraserburg, in the remote Karoo. It is a town destined to be as famous as Paris, Texas, once the movie is made. We looked out from the cool veranda to the sweltering desert, where a flock of kestrels swirled in the heat on *ah! bright wings*. The lamb is reared on the surrounding desert succulents, where the finest specimens in the country frolic.

Tear open the deboned shoulders. Stuff them with a mix of minced lamb and pork into which you have pummelled garlic, crushed walnuts, raisins, cinnamon sticks, lavender, cumin and cardamom seeds. Splash with honey. Tie them up, douse in olive oil, Maldon and black pepper, and bake as slowly as possible until the meat is falling apart. Towards the end smother them in yogurt. The juices and aromas transport you to the harem of a thousand and one nights.

Serve with couscous made with the juices from the pot. Garland the dish with lavender, ideally plucked from Lawrence's fertile desert garden.

Family Supper

So much for restaurants. All you need to do is run one to be put off for the rest of your life. If you ever have another chance at life, and wonder what you might do differently, you now know what to avoid.

Yet, once more, there is always another perspective. Look at eating in the suburbs, perhaps, and you will see why restaurants are justified.

The Old Man gets back from work, smelling of office and suit. He is yawning as he takes his place at the table. He is drinking a beer in a wrap-around lino cooler.

His wife has looked at her watch half an hour earlier, and sighed heavily. She has thrust something brown and smothered in yellow cheese into the microwave.

The son is staring at the television on the melamine

kitchen bar. The daughter has bad spots, and her eyes roll back in her head. She is sipping an orange coloured synthetic drink (diet version) out of a plastic mug.

Another happy supper for the family.

The Pyrex dish has been put on the hot tray. Nobody talks. The TV blares, and eyes flicker from the screen to the plates of congealed brown muck. Lights are bright and unforgiving. ('It's bad for your eyes to watch TV in the dark.') There are plastic table mats with garish flower patterns.

You can't call this eating any more than what might follow can be called sex. (No dear, I have a headache.) It is a mulching process, more like going to the lavatory.

What the family should do is slit their throats. Alternatively, go to bed early and chomp crisps under the blankets. Takeaway pizza too. Takeaway lives.

Two refreshingly contrasting memories. A Spanish family in Malaga on a glorious summer night, around eleven, arriving for supper. The *tapas* spread before them, they embrace and kiss and laugh, everybody touches. The youngest children are five or six, and they chat and laugh as loud as anyone. They hold small glasses of wine, and their lips are stained purple with it. Then, on the banks of the Seine in the moonlight, couples tangoing to music from an old portable record player. None are young, and some are ancient, yet they move with sensual fire. The remains of their simple supper on the quayside: cheeses fresh from the market, crisp baguettes, and flagons of wine.

Hamburger

'How do you make a hamburger?' plaintively asked one of my young friends.

For a moment my instinct was to slap her playfully on the bottom; what could be more simple or straightforward? Then I checked myself; memory intruded. I remembered my own hopeless ineptitude, believing, as I did when young, that food simply happened. It appeared on one's plate as if by divine right. In any event, somebody else knew the secret. It was only once I began to translate my interest in eating into the effort of preparation that I discovered how simple it is. There is no secret, just a few basic procedures, most of them dictated by common sense and natural taste. The brouhaha surrounding the mythology of cooking is codswallop. It is all mystique, and to puncture it you simply need to bung something in the oven. Anyone with a palate can make the effort to do it, and it turns out pretty fine.

When it comes to hamburgers, and my young friend's query, the matter is complicated by the factor of junk food, that is, what hamburgers seem to the young. Here, too, I have a dicky past. I, too, have slavered before the idol McDonald. I have even had the temerity to compare it to Burger King in Leicester Square. Indeed, over a shameful, but mercifully short, period, my first call after landing at Heathrow would be for a Big Mac. My reckless addiction was exacerbated by the fact that McDonald's boycotted the old South Africa, so a certain forbidden lustre piqued the curiosity.

I was instantly cured when I made the error one early morning in Baker Street of stuffing down a second Big Mac on top of the first. It instantly turned. I felt wretched and never touched one again. After the simple effort of making one's own, there is no possible reason to do so. The good old-fashioned hamburger, home-made, is hard to beat.

Get the best lean mince you can find; better, get the butcher to mince beef freshly for you. Cater about 100 grams per burger. Mash some fine-cut onion, salt, pepper and Dijon mustard into the beef (add capers if you like), and bang it into patties the right size for the rolls, which should be soft. Then grill or pan-fry the patties, turning them over low heat until they are cooked through but not overdone. Butter the rolls and plop the burgers inside. Add finely cut gherkin, fresh tomato, tomato sauce and mayonnaise if you wish, or any other condiment that appeals. Skip the limp lettuce leaf.

You will never return to McDonald's again.

Pilaf

This is a hotchpotch of a dish, useful as a disguise for using up leftover bits of meat. The combinations of meat do not really matter: bits of chicken, lamb, beef, duck . . . whatever needs using up before it goes to the dogs.

It is a rice-based dish, so fry up the rice in olive oil and butter with a browned onion. Add stock and let it simmer away. Slice a selection of peppers, onion, carrots and courgettes. Braise them in olive oil, and add to the rice. Throw in some nuts of your choice (cashews or almonds are best, not of course peanuts), raisins, and a handful of crushed spices, such as cardamom, cumin and fenugreek, a squeeze of lemon or lime. Add saffron if you like. Bang them about and add the shredded meats. Cook until the vegetables are *al dente* and the dish is dry.

Top with yogurt, crushed garlic and fresh mint.

Declining years

There is nothing as dispiriting as birthdays, unless you are under twenty-five. I remember my terminal decline into misery as thirty struck. I thought it was all over, as a haunted photograph taken of me staring into the abyss of the swimming pool betrays. The swimming pool stared back into me. There is nothing further to celebrate. One year less to indulge the appetites. One less decadent *confit*, one less succulent lover (or should that be the other way around?).

A friend had a poignant party. The invitation read:

My Fiftieth Birthday

Ideal party
The place – A chateau on the Loire.
The food – Surprise menu specially prepared by Michelin chefs, and served by French waitresses in silk stockings and tiny tight skirts. Grand Cru wines and Kristal.
The guests – Two hundred of my closest friends, flown in by private jet.
The music – Paulo Conte comes by helicopter from Paris. Leonard Cohen jets in. The Berlin Philharmonic renders Beethoven's Ninth. Jessie Norman sings.

Possible party
The place – Daniel's bistrot.
The food – Poached oysters, Langoustines, Crème brûlée.
The guests – Fifty friends, one for each year.
The music – Paulo Conte and Leonard Cohen on CD. String Quartet from the Music School plays Beethoven.

Reality party
The place – My back stoep.
The food – Braai (BYO *wors* and beers).
The guests – Probably only you will turn up.
The music – I've got some old Leonard LPs. You got a turntable and speakers?

Sudden Death Fritters

Up at Clogged Artery Farm, only the arterially tough survive the indulgence of the daily fare. Some arrive young and hearty, only to depart with pacemakers grinding. The Widow smiles her crafty Mona Lisa smile, and touches nothing herself.

Grate some potatoes with hints of carrot and onion. Mix with flour, salt and pepper, a touch of sugar, baking powder, olive oil, and an egg per person. Flatten out into fritters and fry in olive oil.

Mix mascarpone with balsamic vinegar, and smear over the hot cooked fritters. Top them with rolls of smoked salmon and pesto sauce.

The colour combination is most satisfying, set off by serving on a delicate blue plate. One or two guests will drop to the floor in spasm, but it will be a great way to go.

Last Suppers

It seems appropriate to conclude a section on *hors d'oeuvres* with a gesture towards last things. For, if you think about it, the seed of the one is contained in the other. Just as a meal progresses remorselessly from starter to dessert, so too do we. There is that depressing *memento mori* about the days of the week representing decades of one's life. Born on the Monday, we die on the Sunday. So as one drifts through one's forties, it's suddenly Friday morning, and the weekend looms. We eat, we die. We don't eat, we die. So, eat. And make the most of the last weekend.

The sense of eating as a last thing is concentrated in the minds of the condemned on the last evening on death row. The mind must be pretty mixed up at that stage anyway, and one can hardly imagine that it turns delectably to food. That is probably the last thing on the mind. Nevertheless, the tradition persists, at least in the minds of the uncondemned, that a last supper should conjure up a final ecstatic fantasy. Depressing for last supper fantasisers is that the death row inmate in America is offered a choice between a burger and Kentucky fried chicken as the fabled last request. This depresses me more about American taste than it does about capital punishment.

I think the point about a last supper is that it is not

The villa in Lucca on a star-spangled night by the pool

only the food that counts, but the surroundings and conditions in which it takes place. This is a truth about all meals, and an index that restaurants bring to the fore, but the final acid test is on death row. There it might seem most appropriate to make do with that miserable burger, even if one could not force down the fries.

So, to dream up a last supper in the sense of the best meal of one's life, divorce the sense from death row. This is equally true of terminal illness. Sometimes we think of saving the best until last: that tin of Beluga, that bottle of Yquem. Snaffle them at once, do not delay, for one day it will inevitably be too late. There is nothing as nauseating as the prospect of food, even ordinary fare, when one is ill, or, as we say, not feeling up to it. Linda never recovered from her grandmother feeding her soup swimming in oil when she had chickenpox, and I will never forget the expression of nausea, and regret, on a friend's face as he waved away the mussels picked fresh from the rocks, once his favourite dish, in the last stages of his illness. One has to feel up to a great meal, indeed be at a peak of imaginative, and every other kind of health and vivacity. The point about great food is its upward, elevating, enhancing aspects that make it out of the ordinary, aspiring to the sublime, memorable. And memories are made to last.

For your last great supper, you would have to consider the setting and the company as much as the food, for each would influence the other. It is doubtful that one would want to be on one's own, unless the last supper were a misanthropist's. Would the food then have to be miserable?

I would pick the company with great care, and circumspection. People have some practice of this as they celebrate – if celebrate is the word – their great ages, each decade a resounding let-down from the last. Even one's friends appear duller, flabbier, less palatable. I believe one should, in all conscience – indeed taste –

stop pretending to celebrate at an early age, when life still lies ahead, bursting with prospect, while friends are still beautiful and amusing, the palate unalloyed. Ah, those wasted birthday parties as children! (What a nightmare they were.)

My choice would certainly be to have my last meal with the one love of my life, whoever she was at that moment, and eschew the rest. I would hope she would be the ultimate lover, and that, for once, the best would be reserved for last. I would combine the meal with every form of sexual pleasure, not to say depravity, assuming, of course, that I was still up to it. The regrettable truth is that sexual appetite declines along with other failing senses, and that what one is bound to be left with are only memories of former glories when it was all at a rapturous peak. There's no fun in what lies ahead.

I have made the effort to cheer myself up on birthdays with gatherings of friends. This can work, except that one finds that one does all the work. Not only the food, which elicits mumbles of appreciation, but cheering everybody else up too. I find that I am the life and soul of my own party. My guests, who ought to be there to entertain me, at least take my mind off the attrition of years, eagerly (or pitifully) look to me for wit and wisdom, as they plunge their forks remorselessly in and out of their mouths. I have become renowned, or I might say notorious, as the court jester who is bound to offend at least some with his scabrous humour. I put on Tom Waits at full blast, and begin stacking the dishes. How are there always so many? It is all very tedious, and I must give it up (before they all give me up). I will shuffle off to Paris, alone, and devour a *confit* at La Fayette with a bottle of Romanée Conti, and tell myself stories nobody understands. I might even laugh at my own jokes. It may not be my last supper, but it will feel like it.

So much for company. Place and setting are vital, so I will make more ebullient effort in describing these.

They can make or break the meal, and must in any event chime in with what one has to eat. My essentially romantic temperament sways me in the direction of the sea, rivers, mountains, but these are not easy places to indulge a great meal. It is like making love on the beach, or in a forest; sand and pine needles in awkward places, and insects stinging the thighs. Even picnics are hell. No, the setting must be comfortable, private, and depending on the company, as seductive as possible. But then I've done away with company, haven't I? Turn the lights up, at least you can see what you're eating.

I've lived in some beautiful places, and so have my friends. It is to those, or an ideal integration of those, that I would turn for my ideal setting. These are images that return. My godparents' farm in Magoebaskloof, as it was in my memories of childhood. Our apartment in Bruges, perched as high as a cathedral above the canals, swans drifting by. Giles and Nessie's villa in Lucca, on a star-spangled night by the pool, with a quartet playing, stars and candlelight glittering in the water. Gail's mountain fastness, virgin forest and sunset tinting the Outeniqua mountains, ringed by rhino and screened by zebra, as Provençal as paradise. Our *mas* in Provence, rosé wines, tapenades and olives in the courtyard in summer, the cool breath of ancient stones and the ghost in the chapel. Marco's bush camp in Timbavati, the fire flickering in the boma, with only the cries of the wild for company. And Venice *sempre*, and Paris *toujours*, cities for lovers, not only of food.

The great, last supper itself is problematic. One swings between opposite yens: comforting simplicity, of the kind that invariably draws us back to childhood and home, or luxury, bordering on fantasy. I think that both have a claim that is deep and final. On the one hand, there is nothing as good in my memory as my mother's bacon and eggs, usually reserved for Sunday evenings when I

It may not be my last supper, but it will feel like it

was a child. The magic was partly that it was my mother who made it, and she seemed to put all of her love into it, and partly that she concentrated on getting it just right. That meant that the bacon was to a crispiness that did not sacrifice succulence, the fat was neatly trimmed away, the eggs were done at the last moment with the softness ratio of yolk to white perfect, the fried bread scrumptious. So, like Francis Bacon, who wanted only a boiled egg with bread and butter for his last supper, simplicity counts, but it must be perfect.

On the upper end, the fantasy scale, this is my last supper:

Fresh Foie Gras
Fresh Crayfish
Tarte Tatin with Crème Fraiche

Otherwise, for most suppers, each one of which may be the last, I settle for chubby, in all of his comforting guises.

2

MEMORIES

Feast in Venice

Every tourist asks the concierge for his recommendation of restaurant, and always adds, *sotto voce*, 'Where the locals eat, nothing touristy.' This is the familiar quest for fool's gold and nobody who has travelled much expects the response to pander to more than wishful thinking.

Nowhere is this disillusioning ritual played out more often and with less masking than in Venice, the most seductive and most treacherous tourist trap in the world. So it was with wryness that I put the question, hardly disguising the rules of the game which admit to defeat in advance. It is challenging to match the cynicism of the Venetians with that of one's own. I won't say the concierge looked less guileful than anticipated but his directions were peculiarly detailed and complicated. It wasn't a matter of shooing us around the corner following the lights, but appearing to take trouble to guide us into a labyrinth with some scrupulousness. Perhaps he took a shine to Linda, who looked radiant on the second last night of one of our many prolonged honeymoon romances.

We groped our way, finally seeing the sign on a dark square. The door was closed on this spring evening and we opened it to the glare of a restaurant packed to the rafters, vibrant with smoke and animated chatter. All Italian; not a thin English nor fat American voice in the place. The maitre d', formal in white jacket and braid, gave a look of undisguised hostility, as though we were out of place. We were of course, but then he saw *la bella* Linda which brought out the true Italian in him.

We were jammed at a table surrounded by Venetians in various stages of engorgement; dinner in Italy is a serious affair and foreigners are scorned who take it lightly. It is not possible, and certainly not in a proper restaurant, to make do with a pasta and eschew the courses which both precede and follow. It is awkward to get away with less than four courses, of which the main is the third. Ever wary of our pathetic currency – and knowing that to eat in Italy was far more expensive than, say, in France – we picked modestly and clearly did not impress the maitre d'. The fare was absolutely standard: a little scampi to start, pasta, a bit of veal, cassata. It tasted as ordinary as countless such rote meals do all over Italy – their only virtue being the feeling that one is in Italy itself, as if the place lends savour to the food – and it cost more than usual.

The point of the evening was located elsewhere: at the adjacent table. There we noticed fare nothing like our own, nor like anything we could identify on the menu. Platter after platter of delicacies arrived, exquisite, mysterious, redolent of the deep secrets of *la Serenissima*. Every one looked so tantalising that had we been in familiar territory, or tipsier, we might have reached out a finger to press a succulent titbit to our lips. As it was, we watched with Oliver Twist pangs of envy as the maitre d' himself flashed to and fro executing bows and flourishes. We particularly noted at one point in the feast, which the blessed couple tore into with abandon, that a glass of wine of subtle flamingo hue was ceremoniously offered to the maitre d', who rolled it round his mouth with ceremonial gravity.

So it was that, overcome with the glory of what we had seen and not tasted, and by the beguiling romance of that intoxicated city, we stammered and gesticulated to the maitre d' that we would like to be presented the following night, our last in the city, with exactly the feast we had just witnessed. It was only as we walked briskly back to the hotel that it occurred to us that we had neglected to enquire as to the cost. *Alora!* This was the romance of Venice after all!

The next night we took the boat all the way up the Grand Canal and back, the most romantic journey in the world and worth repeating endlessly. In fact it took longer than we remembered so we dashed to the restaurant, panting and desperate, an hour late. Of course it was full, the vibrancy of the night before provoking a sense of terrible regret. We were confronted, shamefaced, by the fierce maitre d' and bowed and scraped our apologies. *Presto!* With a disarming flourish he directed our gaze to one lone table obscured in the middle of the packed room. The small plaque read *riservato*. Had we been Italians we would have kissed him on both cheeks.

Then commenced the finest feast ever savoured. We were delirious, that is my excuse for the blurring of memory between one delicacy and the next, one voluptuous sensation and the next, the sense that it could go on for ever. Everything was of the sea and much we could not identify, crustacea, claws and tendrils, bursting with fresh tangs of the Adriatic. At what we took to be the salient moment, we too called for an extra glass and proffered the flamingo elixir to the maitre d' and basked in his appreciation.

A point to make is that the perfections and subtleties in taste were matched visually. Our gaze was as riveted to the food as were our tastebuds wildly stimulated. Only once did we look up, gratified to see a party of Americans being turned away – *completo* – late in the evening when there were plainly many vacant tables. We felt very special indeed, sharing vicariously the camaraderie of the locals rejecting the vulgar intruders.

It had to end. The last tentacle or tendril slipped down the gullet. We looked at each other, glowing with a hundred tantalising flavours and textures. What price paradise? Buoyed by the ecstasy of the feast, we felt that even if it cost, say, ten times the amount of the night before – which would make it astronomical, more than the whole week's meals – it would, well, just be worth it. Anyway it was too late. We had felt it a vulgarity to have enquired anxiously halfway through what it might be costing, as if we would demean not only ourselves but the feast itself, and preferred to, as it were, go down in style. This was the moment to regret our panache. I fondled the credit card with damp palm.

As is usual in Italy, the presentation of the bill is a nerve-racking and incomprehensible affair. At the due moment the waiter sidles to the table, creases his brow with the effort of memory, and proceeds to scrawl with lightning speed a long list – much longer than you recall devouring – of squiggles, all of which end in a frightening number of zeros. It may only be lira (in the old days) but it's millions. The indecipherable bit of paper is upside down on the saucer and he glowers above you. This is not the moment to make a run for it.

We were determined not to let our savoir-faire crack, but it nearly did. Our man scribbled for ten minutes. Mustering a brave grin, and encouraging Linda to show a sliver more of thigh, I turned the bill over. It came to exactly the amount we had paid for the perfectly ordinary meal the night before.

I'll never know if it was a miracle or a mistake. We tried to find out what we had eaten but language failed. Perhaps what we had eaten defied description. What we did learn was that we would have to wait another year before we might enjoy such a meal again. It was the spring tide and only then does the sea disgorge the deep mysterious rareties and nuances that had made this night almost untranslatable.

Pasta for Every Occasion

Pasta is one of the essential staples, and you don't have to be Italian to be addicted. For me, it assumes higher priority than rice, potato or polenta. I could not do without it, as a dish on its own with its myriad forms, or as an accompaniment to a meal. It is versatile and adapts brilliantly to a host of flavours.

First essential is to select the right pasta. The cardinal rule is to go for the Italian makes, usually the more expensive the better. Don't touch the local brands which turn instantly to wallpaper glue. Approach local home-made or part-fresh brands with caution. If they are made in Bellville or Isando, that is warning enough. Pasta is a proud Italian tradition, and if you are not in Italy, cannot get an Italian to make it fresh for you, and cannot even bother making it yourself (make sure you get the flour right), then stick to the Italian in a box.

Second essential is to cook it right. That means undercooking it, only just. The Italians say *al dente*, which means *to the tooth*. So the test is to extract a piece from the boiling water and bite it. You must feel the bite, and it is ready at the moment the hard core in the centre is cooked through. A moment later and it is ruined. The other way of testing its readiness is to hurl a piece at the wall. The moment it sticks, it's done. This is a method I often prefer, and Ollie adopts it with gusto. It tends to enrage the fastidious and the anally retentive.

Pasta must be rapidly boiled in lots of water, salted, so that it does not stick together and turn out mush. Separate it out as it starts to boil, then leave it alone.

You can add almost anything you fancy to pasta. I recommend caution and simplicity. Do not gild the lily. Choose

You don't have to be Italian to be addicted

something, and exclude others until next time. The more you mix in, the worse it will be.

The finest pasta I ever enjoyed, we made late one freezing night in a Paris flat where we could lay our hands only on a box of spaghetti, olive oil, sea salt, and the window box in which only the thyme survived. A sprinkling of parmesan (again here, go for the real thing, or as close to it as you can find; substitutes and all the grated varieties will make you puke), and we had perfect simplicity, or simple perfection. It is amazing how much you can wolf down on a winter's night with a bottle of red. Pasta is for atmosphere.

Here are some other favourites, but it is easy to make up your own.

Pasta with Sage
The trick is to lightly crisp the sage leaves in butter. Do not burn the butter or the leaves. They are done just as they curl up crisply. Add nothing but parmesan to the pasta, and gobbets of butter.

Pasta with Smoked Salmon & Crème Fraiche
No cooking here at all. Simply stretch the whole leaves of salmon over the pasta on the plate, screw black pepper, add a squeeze of lemon if you like, and put a good blob of crème fraiche in the centre. Italians tend not to add parmesan to pasta with fish, but I don't see why not.

Pasta with Ham & Mushrooms
Any mushroom goes wonderfully well with pasta; it must be the textures that blend so sensuously on the tongue. Mushrooms can be cooked with garlic and pepper, and they are ready when the liquid that they exude in the pan dries up. Toss them into the pasta with olive oil and strips of ham, parma ham is naturally the finest. Don't resist the temptation to add crème fraiche.

Pasta with Pine Rings

As the first rains of autumn fall, make for the forests and gather mushrooms. Don't put it off for another day, mushrooms are cruel and can disappear far too quickly for another year's hibernation before you can gird your loins.

I choose pine rings because they are the likeliest you will find in any quantity. But of course pasta is as delicious, even more so, with ceps (the *edulis*) or the elusive Prince, which Peter ferrets out surreptitiously on autumn mornings in the Elgin woods before anyone can get to them, then wolfs them down for breakfast.

Dust and slice the mushrooms (avoid washing) – the scent of wild mushrooms is one of their enticements – and fry in olive oil, with garlic and rashers of bacon if you like. Add thick cream, salt and pepper, and mix into the pasta.

Pasta with Bacon and Clams

This is a delicious combination. Start frying slices of streaky bacon and garlic. As it crisps, add a good glug of olive oil, black pepper, and clams that you have squeezed the juice out of. While the clams are sizzling, add parsley to fry, then a tin of tomatoes, a pinch of sugar, splodge of red wine, and tomato paste. Turn the heat down, and let this thick sauce simmer away for longer than you would think, so that the ingredients are well steeped. Toss the sauce over the pasta, and top with parmesan, hunks of mozarella, and parsley.

Pasta Carbonara

This is a well-loved favourite, perhaps because it is reminiscent of bacon and eggs, that most tempting of breakfasts, and one good thing the English have contributed to our sense of well-being, at least in the mornings. It is probably the most commonly home-made pasta apart from the often abused spaghetti bolognese, which is usually tasteless, sloppy and stale, redolent of boarding school smells, or something left in the warmer to coagulate and turn grey overnight.

Fry up the bacon as you like it, with garlic, dice and throw into the pasta. The eggs must be whisked firmly and tossed raw into the hot pasta. They will lightly scramble quite naturally, and add a delectable silky richness to the texture. Add olive oil, parmesan, black pepper and Maldon to crunch on top.

Pasta Salsiccia
Back in Germany after some years, I am struck with conflicting elements once more. There is a darkness in the architecture and the grey-green colours that is somewhat grim and foreboding, a heaviness that oppresses; yet there is a lightness and politeness in the cheery, hygienic openness of the people that lifts the spirit. The weather's been like that too, grey skies broken by shafts of summer light.

There is no more sensual buoyancy than in the laughter and vitality of my sexy friend Coco, whose zest is infectious, even rousing a wolfish grin from her partner, the saturnine *Führer,* Kris. Coco cooks pasta like only a good German could: with all the passion of an Italian.

Her pasta *salsiccia piccante* gives a revitalising lift to the idea of sausage, the ingredient that permeates German cuisine. Here, the sausage is vibrant and vermilion, as only one from the heady mountains of Italy could be. It is peppery and spicy, bursting with the vigour of the Dolomites.

It needs to be attacked with a large sharp knife, slit down the middle, then several long cuts to shred it like a banana, and diced into small bite pieces. Fry it up with diced onions and garlic in olive oil, and add a scoop of pesto. Coco, exotic creature that she is, uses a subtle dandelion pesto that she finds in a health food store in Düsseldorf. Add a couple of tins of whole Italian tomatoes and a sprinkle of nutmeg. Serve with tagliatelle and plenty of fresh grated *parmigiano reggiano*.

Pasta with Prunes
This is an odd, but delicious combination, a recipe Coco picked up in Florence.

Fry up in olive oil, garlic with peperoncini, which are small dried chilli peppers (you might have to use fresh chillies instead). Toss in tins of Italian tomatoes and a handful of dried prunes which you tear into pieces, nutmeg, and what Coco, in her sultry German accent, pronounces a 'zip' of red wine, simmer (or zimmer) and reduce. Take off the heat, and add mozzarella slices (find the real buffalo if you can, it is immeasurably superior), so that the cheese merges softly, but does not melt like sticky plastic. Toss over pasta, and smother in parmesan.

On the last night we spent together, Coco wickedly contrived a pasta of the most exquisite simplicity. She grated fine slivers of fresh truffle, which she'd sniffed out in the market, over the spaghetti, with a dash of olive oil. You, too, will want to spend the rest of your life with Coco, for a zip of zexy zest.

Blue Duck at La Tour d'Argent

The undistinguished skyscraper on the left bank opposite Notre Dame in Paris enshrines one of the best restaurants in the world. *La Tour d'Argent* settles serenely at the pinnacle of the building, the reinforced glass dome affording a gaze of superior disdain over the mere bistrots, cafés and two star Michelin restaurants that grovel below.

The Michelin ratings are the most keenly contested, coveted, and strenuously defended culinary accolades in the world, particularly to the French who established them. They did so with ruthless, self-serving Gallic savvy, which the world, largely, has bought into. (Should you not adhere to Michelin, consult Gault Milau.) For of all the tens of thousands of restaurants in France, and the millions that might qualify for the attention of the Michelin inspectors worldwide – imagine it – only a handful are accorded the supreme honour of three stars, the greatest proportion in Paris, naturally. There might be a grudging qualifier now and then outside France, but that is in virtue of their aspiring to be French. The rest of the world *n'existe pas*. It is there only to grovel in reverence and envy.

The same trick has worked of course with wine, where the French have accorded to themselves the accreditation for all the finest wines in the world, simply on the assumption that no others count. The best wines in the world are Chateaux d'Yquem, Lafite, Latour, Haut Brion and Mouton Rothschild. That's it, *mon frère, viva liberté*, and stuff *égalité*.

Michelin inspectors tramp the cities and byways of the country, often coming up with obscure and esoteric commendations. There are critics who believe the enterprise too elitist and, in some sense, arbitrary for its own good (and some restaurateurs even give the inspectors short shrift, to their inevitable exclusion). Nonetheless, it is akin to a Booker Prize or Oscar nomination: an establishment can rise from obscurity to acclamation at the scratch of a pen. Some renowned chefs are always included, and their emporia are luxurious and attentive to detail in ways that exemplify Michelin meticulousness. It may not be everyone's taste, or best method of ranking, but it has the cachet and it is, in my limited experience, a high standard to go by. I don't quarrel with it. In fact, I admire the sureness of its supreme arrogance, the flair with which it arrogates the rest to oblivion. And if we're gullible enough to buy it, so much the better for it. *Viva la France!* We should surely be the poorer without it.

This prelude is designed to put as forcefully as possible the sense of hallowed awe that surrounds the Michelin ethos. The award of one star, even the breath of recommendation, is a rare and singular distinction, 'an especially good restaurant in its class'. Two is only for the archangels of the kitchen, 'excellent cooking, worth a detour'. Three, 'exceptional cuisine, worth a special journey'.

Restaurateurs will kill – or die – for it. This is no idle metaphor. Recently, Bernard Loiseau, whose restaurant,

Lameloise, was one of the most acclaimed in Burgundy, committed suicide when he lost a star, and plummeted into mere First Class from his stratospheric Concorde three star status. To hobnob with the hoi polloi in First was too much to bear, and the *maître* took the carver to his own throat, as any noble Michelin superchef surely would. Pity, since I have actually eaten there, and it was faultless.

As a measure of the seriousness accorded food and its accreditation, a recent attack on the system published by a disillusioned Michelin inspector, accusing the organisation of nepotism and inadequate policing, has caused apoplexy in French gastronomic circles. Michelin defended its sacrosanctity by effectively labelling the whistle-blower an enemy of the state. The Michelin star is the symbol of the country itself.

La Tour d'Argent is perhaps the longest entrenched and most famous of the Michelin three stars. It is not without a daunting aspect, as was made plain the moment we stepped into the lift that soars to heaven. The purpose of the lift, which stops a couple of times on the way up, is not merely to save the corpulent the flights of stairs. No rich person wants to walk. It has a more cunning purpose, quintessentially French in its ingenious deviousness. The real purpose of the lift is to screen the customers.

An intimidating commissionaire, decked out as an admiral, casts an eye over you at every stage of the journey. What they are looking for are signs not only of indigence (it is not possible to wash the dishes as recompense for not paying), but sartorial inadequacy. It is necessary not only to have the means, and the stomach, for the best restaurant in the world, but to look the part.

Being French, the first appraising look is to the feet. The French are obsessive about shoes, the correct footwear for the occasion, and the more expensive the designer the better. Hand-made English shoes are the acme. I believe it would be de rigueur to walk stark naked into the Ritz wearing only a pair of Church brogues.

The groundfloor commissionaire's gaze swept from our feet upwards over every centimetre of clothing to our heads. I think a buzzer sounded discreetly. At the first stop we were politely (but firmly) whisked from the lift. Blue blazer and striped tie were produced. Another flunkey dressed us appropriately. We were scrutinised afresh. A whisper and glances exchanged. We resumed our journey to the stars.

It was amusing to see, as we were finally ushered into the hallowed space, twenty other guests identically decked out like Onassis on a yacht in blue blazers and striped ties. (They are stripped off you as you leave – as a final, again perfectly French, insult to injury.)

What is most intimidating about such absurdly pretentious restaurants is the waiters. Although to think of them as waiters is quite beyond one's sense of daring. They are more like Eton headmasters in the days when they could bend you over the block for a beating. There is no doubt whatsoever that you are in their territory, and you'd better believe it. You are lucky to be there. For as long as you behave properly. And of course pay the equivalent of a poor country's gross national product. Nowhere is the gap between rich and poor, them and us, more apparent, nor more disdainfully reinforced. It is only the very rich who can stomach it.

The waiters hover menacingly. There are battalions of them and they do not leave you alone for a moment. We deferentially ordered the restaurant's most famous dish, the pressed duck. We did not really know what we were doing.

The duck is strangled and left to fester in its blood, then eaten raw as it falls apart. That is a slight misrepresentation, but that is what it tastes like. *Le canard bleu*. The duck is blue-grey and looks old and miserable, as well it might. It is forced down with some resistance. It costs the equivalent of a duck farm. The wine – the only bottle remotely affordable, but the very best are there – we sipped with a sense of reverence, and bewilderment. We declined the cognacs which could be matched, at a stellar price, to the year of one's birth. We handed back our Onassis kit at the door with some relief, ending if not the most overrated, then certainly the most undercooked, meal in the world.

Steak Tartare and Wagner

When I arrived as a postgraduate student in Cambridge, and saw my tutor for the first time, I thought I had stepped into *Butley*, the Simon Gray play which Alan Bates had made memorable at the time. He stood in a fug of scented cigarettes and eau de cologne, tight pigskin pants and cherry red pullover, teetering precariously between piles of books and records that were scrambled from floor to ceiling. I could just make out tousled red hair and jumping eyebrows amid the chaos of the room. I expected him to imitate Butley's vomiting rejection of an intrusive student, but he radiated a puckish smile and beckoned me in.

Thus began an intoxicating academic sojourn in Cambridge, where I commenced my doctoral studies. Michael was a passionate exponent of the Total Experience when it came to teaching, drawn from his hero Richard Wagner's conception of the Total Work of Art. Teaching, too, aspired to the condition of music, that is, music as an all-embracing, ecstatic world view.

It all seems rather passé now, but to the impressionable student, it made a forceful impact. Michael gathered acolytes who lasted only as long as they were in the master's thrall. One was the music while the music lasted.

When it came to food, though, the pretensions of high

art, moral seriousness, vivacity and the rest, were abandoned, and Michael reverted to the plainness of a fireman's son. Stodgy nosh from the Whim or Grad Pad would be stuffed down without ceremony. The important issue was not the food, but not to waste time before returning to the great debates and the *Liebestod*. It was only if food could be in some way perfectly combined with the Wagnerian way of life that it might matter. That happened only once, and it does qualify as one of the great moments in which food and art reached catharsis, simultaneous orgasm.

You have to transport yourself to the setting. Ancient rooms in a medieval college, redolent with the vapours of great learning, autumn mists and clanging church bells. Inside, behind heavy drawn curtains and a stout oak door, a heady amalgam of high art, mellow lighting and gas fire flickering, heroism and decadence. The master swaying in rapture as the music swells, dwarfed by pictures of the giants, Wagner, Mahler, and Wilhelm Furtwängler. No wonder the young were impressed!

For the supreme experience, the food had to attain the raptures of the gods. Michael found the ideal combination, complete in its simplicity and seriousness. Steak tartare, made freshly with all the trappings from the best fillet the butcher had that afternoon, washed down with a chilled bottle of sparkling burgundy. The perfect rawness of authenticity, and the vivacity of the wine: *Tristan* in a meal.

Spider Crabs out of the Garage

My friends Jane and Nikos are the most exotic couple in ways that seem quintessentially French, although neither is. She is English by birth, although temperamentally a child of the universe, a *natuurkind* with an always refreshing bohemian élan. That was why they met. Janie

A spectacle to make Neptune caper for joy: Linda, Nikos and his children

was sailing single-handedly round the world – if she is bohemian, she also has enough nous to launch a flotilla of yachts – and landed on a deserted beach in Cayenne. Deserted except for the Robinson Crusoe-like figure of Nikos, berry tanned, stretched out in a hammock, and gazing at the lovely mermaid creature emerging from her yacht, golden hair in ringlets to her coccyx. He had been like that for a year, and it appeared, suddenly, that he was transfixed by the image of the sea nymph. In fact, he was contemplating his next move in the Japanese game of Gó.

As Nikos, who is Polish by origin, but French to the roots of his mad tousled hair, explained to me much later, the game of Gó is the game of games for the simple reason that it has no rules. It is exactly like life, except that you may not commit suicide. More accurately, it is a game of life and death, and to play one game might take a week or a year. It might take your life.

Jane and Nikos live in Paris now, where he is a distinguished physicist and she a sculptor and teacher, and every summer holiday they go to a farmhouse in Brittany, which is a great relief from the maniacal hordes of Parisians who make relentlessly for the south coast and the intolerable heat and crowds of the Riviera. Brittany, even in the teeth of summer, has a bucolic mellowness which is enchanting. And the main point is the crustaceans, and the curious way in which one comes across them.

Nikos gave nothing away as we puttled through the village in his clapped-out car. Like all good Frenchmen, he brushes aside the car as a necessary irrelevance, its purpose to get one around with as much slapdash speed as possible. 'What are bumpers for?' he said nonchalantly as we bashed into the car parked in front of us, and drew up with a jolt outside an ordinary house with a garage. We entered not the house but the garage. And there was no car inside, only great tanks brimming with every imaginable form of crustacean, plucked from the robust coast of Brittany. It was a spectacle to make Neptune caper for joy.

Gorging ourselves on the array of lobsters, mussels, oysters, sea urchins, and – the revelation to me – spider crabs, with the sunlight pouring through the window over the stove where Nikos devotedly plunged them into a boiling pot, is one of the enduringly rapturous memories of my summers in Brittany. The mussels Nikos cooked with the glorious local cider and clotted cream; everything else spoke for itself, fresh, unadorned, and singing of the sea.

After the feast, we and the children danced on the lawn outside to country music, joining hands and kicking our legs high, intoxicated by the sheer magic of being so alive in such a place, the shellfish bubbling in our tummies. They never forgot the last glimpse of me staggering on to the train back to Paris, a shopping bag of live spider crabs writhing in my hand.

> ## Crab
>
> To anyone who has the slightest doubt of the glory of the crab, I commend David Malouf's poem *The Crab Feast*. It will give succulence and relish to your sex life as much as to your next mouthful of crab. This is how it begins:
>
> *There is no getting closer*
> *than this. My tongue slips into*
> *the furthest, sweetest corner*
> *of you. I know all*
>
> *now all your secrets.*
>
> So for your own crab feast, make it a seductive occasion. Start with a throaty rendition of the poem, and the rest will follow naturally.

The point at which the sea touches the heavens

> Select your crab in the ratio of size to weight: the heavier the better. The meat is in the pincers so size them up as if you were a slave trader after the prize specimens. The crab, like any crustacean, should be alive, and the livelier the fresher it is.
>
> Throw it into boiling water for ten minutes or so. The glory of the crab feast is invoking a spirit of voluptuous violence. All you need is an implement which will smash the pincers and one which will assist in prising out the most hidden morsels. No sauce, no accompaniments, no finesse. Go at it with hammer, tongs and fingers, extracting every last sliver of silky delicate flesh. Some violence is not out of place.
>
> Crab is the sweetest of the ocean secrets. It is the point at which the sea touches the heavens.

Crayfish from Mrs Fish

You won't believe it, but the good woman who ran the fish shop was Mrs Fish. Her husband, Mr Fish, looked just like a lightly boiled crayfish. In those days, you rang Mrs Fish and used the code.

'Have you any pies today, Mrs Fish?'

'How many would you like, dear?'

For five rand (in my time – older friends tell me it was once much less), you got a lusty crayfish with a strong thrashing tail. It was a mere formality, then, to walk back from the harbour to the house with the rustling plastic bag, and thrust the creatures into boiling water. How to do it is simple, if brutal. If you have a certain theatrical bent, you might arrange three-legged races to determine which is first into the pot. (I remember when I did this one time, a pale and slender girl declined to eat crayfish at all . . .) I might just add that there is absolutely no reason to adopt the French gourmet finesse of injecting the live crayfish with a spurt of champagne before consigning it to the boil, a superfluous refinement, except perhaps for the frisson of cruelty.

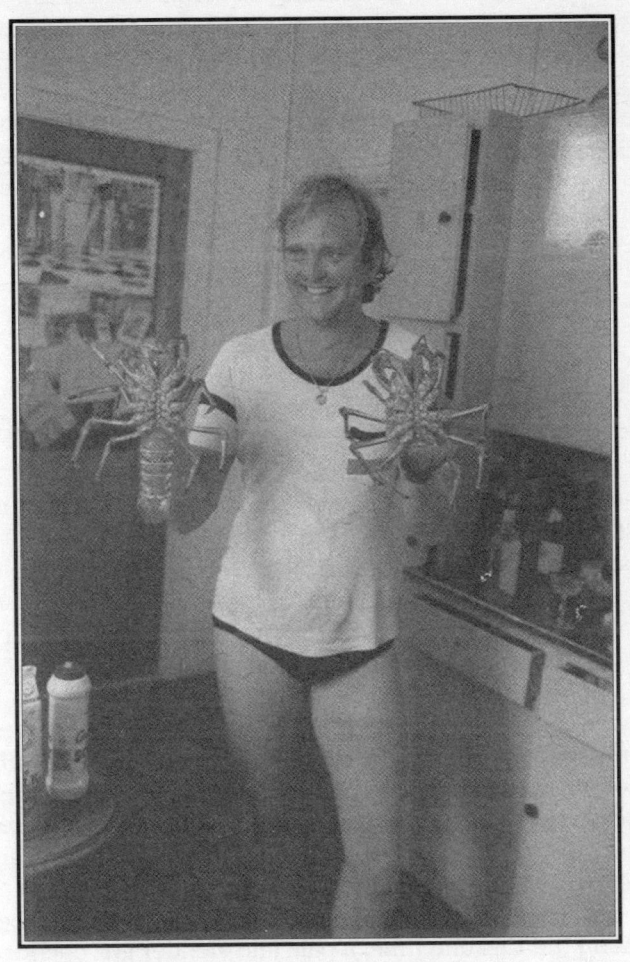

'Any pies today, Mrs Fish?'

I must make mention here of my godson James, and record the one truly enchanting remark of his childhood. I was in my mystery mode when I confronted the little fellow with my writhing packet, stuffed with live crayfish. All he could see and hear was the turbulence inside the packet. He stared, unable to imagine what lurked struggling within. Suddenly, a claw thrust through the packet. James jumped back, wide-eyed.

'Is it a tiger?' he gasped.

Crayfish

The only way to eat crayfish is alive from the sea. There is nothing more perfect than taking it direct from a fishing boat on the beach, the tail thrusting strongly, the scent of the sea, and cooking it at once, over a fire on the beach if you can. If it is dead or frozen it tastes like newspaper. Fresh, it is the most sensual of all crustaceans.

It is, finally and indubitably, my choice of last supper.

The last of the deplorably short season were borne to us on the beach at Paternoster by Coco, the sexiest *fashionista* in Europe, whose stiletto-heeled, thigh-gripping boot collection sends erotic shivers up the spine.

The crayfish are taken fresh from the sea, the more immediate the better, and thrust into the pot of boiling water. Slap the lid down hard, the crayfish will thrash about. Boil until it changes to a radiant burnt umber and curls over. Do not overcook, ten minutes is about right; the firmness of the flesh is essential to the bite.

Run cold water over it so it is comfortable to handle. Break the tail out of the carapace and slit it down the inside centre alongside the dark trail of the intestine. Do not sever the intestine; extract it intact and discard. Sluice out the brown muck in the carapace and put the tail back in place for serving.

Devour the crayfish with a simple sauce such as lemon and butter, perhaps a hint of garlic, but nothing that detracts from

Crayfish tastes of the sex of the sea

the unique delicacy of flavour.

I take the whole tail in my fingers, dip it into the sauce, and slip it down my throat in one lingering thrust. That for me is the sublime moment. The intricate pattern of the flesh impressed within the shell is an astonishing work of art, the mechanical structure of tail and claws is perfect. Relish it slowly. Crack each claw gently and suck out the flesh in an unbroken ribbon. Do not neglect the succulent white flesh behind the eyes. Seek out every morsel in the carapace, ignoring only the grey and brown: every cranny yields its secrets.

Crayfish tastes of the sex of the sea.

Prawns in the Rain & Oysters on the Seine

The enjoyment of shellfish is often enhanced out of doors. It seems appropriate, somehow, the sea and the windswept shore. The closest I've got to perfection in this kind of pathetic fallacy is giant tiger prawns on the braai in a lashing thunderstorm in Parktown North, and oysters slugged back with wine in springtime on the banks of the Seine.

My brother-in-law Connie makes no claim to be one of the world's great cooks, but he can braai a mean prawn. In the rain, *nogal*. We put him out one dismal stormy night as we sheltered serenely under cover, yelling orders. He held an umbrella over his head as the rain lashed down, and looked miserable. It was, in retrospect, a heroic achievement. Those crisp, succulent Mozambique cockroaches of the deep take some beating, and tossed over the flames in the rain as only Connie could do, smothered in butter, lemon and garlic, they are as decadent an indulgence as you might get. We glugged them down with green-tinted Portugese wine, and struggled to put back half a dozen each. I crunch them whole, from the top of the head, down the crisp body, to the spiny legs, relishing every texture. We fell back (indoors) with a sense of wild repletion.

As to the oysters ... remember that their special frisson is that they are a rare delicacy that is ingested alive. They strike the epiglottis with the resonance of vivid life. Some say it is like sperm at the back of the throat. For some reason like this, they are always close to a girl's heart, and are a commonly cited aphrodisiac. Whatever the truth, the oyster is an untranslatable sensation, slurped raw, and without any intermediary cooking. (Although a lightly poached oyster, in champagne particularly, is quite delicious, albeit lacking the spontaneous titillation of aliveness.)

I recall with some despondency poor Mae, who for an unaccountable reason must have lapsed into a pre-sensual stage (from which, happily, she has entirely emerged), and gagged at the very thought of oysters, crying out, like young Augustus, 'I won't have any oysters today, oh take the nasty oysters away', as Linda and I settled in to our fourth or fifth dozen.

They were most serenely plopped down the throat on the banks of the Seine in that most desirable slender riverside park under the Pont Neuf called the Square du Vert Galant. We would roam the street market on rue Montorgueil, and take the oysters down the steps to the river with a bottle of Muscadet. Even though one is not allowed to sprawl on the grass (an officious little Frog blows his whistle), there is no more serene place to slip the oysters down, then exchange oyster kisses as the wide river flows placidly by.

Mussels

It is enticing to pick your own from the rocks at low tide when the mussel beds are exposed above the water. I have done it with many a lover, as it is almost a sexual act in itself. The open mussel suggests, to a more graphic degree, what D H Lawrence saw in the fig, 'the female part, the fissure, the moist conductivity toward the centre'.

There are different attitudes to size. I prefer them medium in the French style and avoid the gobstoppers that stick in the throat.

Mussels are bivalve feeders and certain precautions should be taken before consuming them. Take those that are still under water if you can, and least exposed to the sun. Don't take any that have baked and look dried out. Beware of red tide since mussels absorb the toxin. An infected mussel can kill. It is essential, and not merely preferable like other shellfish, that they are alive when cooked. This means they are tightly closed before cooking and there are no cracks or breaks in the shell. When cooked they must open at once and those that are recalcitrant should be discarded. Never force a mussel.

When you have your sack of mussels — and it is easy to put back a few dozen — put them in a tub of running cold water to filter out the sand. Scrub the seaweed and limpets from the shells.

In the pot singe a diced onion and stick of celery in olive oil until soft but not burnt. Add a glass of white wine and bring to the boil. Throw in the mussels and slap on the lid so they can steam rapidly. After a minute take a look and begin extracting mussels which have opened. They open almost immediately on exposure to the heat and should be taken out at once. Swizz them about to encourage the tardy.

Once the mussels are waiting in the serving dish, add black pepper, chopped parsley and cream to the pot and stir to a good consistency. Toss the sauce over the mussels and serve with thin cut *frites* and baguette. Dijon mustard with the French fries is delicious, and the bread is dunked in the sauce. Avoid English mustard; it is only for those with no palate.

Coquilles St Jacques

The great rival to oysters for supreme seashell sensation is the *coquille* St Jacques, the exquisite shell out of which Venus steps in Botticelli's painting, the classic shell of shells. Its name derives from pilgrims returning to Paris along the rue St Jacques from Compostella in Spain, bringing the lovely shells as a testament from their destination. I hope they devoured the *coquilles* with as much religious fervour as they could muster, for they are one of the supreme subtleties in taste and aesthetic satisfaction.

Coquilles adorn the fishmarkets of Paris in the spring. We would choose according to the beauty of the shell as much as the plumpness of the *coquille*. The plumpness of the coral too, shining orange, is a great asset, and it is a perfectly delicious complement to the virgin, pure white *coquille*. The fishmonger will pull out the gubbins that encases the *coquille* and its coral, and the gift of the sea is borne away to be cooked at once.

It takes half a minute, flipped over in a pan of sizzling butter. Do not cook for longer. You can either cook the coral whole with the *coquilles*, or add it to the sauce and mash it in. For the sauce, add a splash of good white wine or champagne (with a dish of this sublime delicacy, the wine is an investment), and a dash of salt and pepper to the pan once the *coquilles* are out, and whizz with a dollop of crème fraiche. Serve the *coquilles* back in their shells. The sensation is as voluptuous as Venus stepping out of her shell just for you.

Alas, here we find only frozen or tinned *coquilles* which are mingy, tasteless, and bear as much relation to the fresh original as a postcard does to a sculpture of Rodin's. Hold out until you can find them fresh; they are almost worth an eternity.

In Search of the Perfect Confit

It took an unconscionable time for me to discover the voluptuous joy of the *confit de canard*. It is the supreme achievement with the duck, in which the noble creature (just the leg quarter) is preserved in its thick fat over the long winter until, revived in the spring, it melts in the mouth like a buttery thigh. It is enough to make one sink to one's knees with gratitude to the creature

High-speed adrenalin rushes. Rupert on the prowl in Paris

which sacrificed itself to give so much pleasure. Alternatively, it provides a quick means for the cholesterol-challenged to end their miserable days on a note of rapture.

I often troll the streets of Paris searching for the ultimate *confit* (I try to make it coincide with the ultimate *tarte tatin*, so that I can get to heaven in one go). Truth is, not all *confits* are equal, although all are gloriously good. You will never forget your first taste, and you cannot imagine that you will survive the ecstasy. The texture is of a richness, and thickness, that suffuses the mouth with voluptuousness. It is reminiscent of clotted cream or lamb slow cooked until it falls from the bone. Succulence is all. You feel, as the first trembling forkful strikes the gullet, that you are entering the dangerous but irresistible gates of forbidden pleasures. One thinks of Kubla Khan:

And close your eyes with holy dread,
For he on honey-dew hath fed,
And drunk the milk of Paradise.

I have trudged the streets with Mae in the spring rain, when, aching from painting the apartment and lugging stuff up the stairs, only the prospect of another *confit* kept us going. We almost overreached ourselves, and that is not an easy thing for us to do, hardened indulgers and gluttons that we are. Yet, after putting back a *confit* every second night over two weeks, we fortunately saved ourselves from being struck down on the rue La Fayette by enormous infarcti as we hesitated outside the *Général*. We stared at the alluring interior; our waiter was already beckoning like the serpent to Eve; the rain came down. In a sudden depressing recognition of human frailty, we knew we just could not do it. Perhaps it was that the *moules à la marinière* from lunch had not quite settled, perhaps a stronger sense of self-preservation prevailed. We turned away from the *Général* feeling wretched, pusillanimous, buoyed up only by the prospect of surviving for another occasion in a future Paris.

Again, with Rupert, tearing through Paris on the back of his huge motorbike (so intimidating that even the *gendarmes* salute as he speeds by), I controlled my terror only by riveting my thoughts on the ultimate *confit*. I might indulge in a small confession here, and ask the forgiveness of my mother. Her proscriptions against ever getting on to a motorbike are among the strongest imperatives of my youth. I remember being raddled with guilt the one and only time I audaciously got on to Zubby Zev's 49cc *autie*, and let him puttle me round the block. I never got over my mother's motorbike warnings, which seemed to have the force not only of physical concern, but moral law. So, thirty years later, I crave her indulgence for my high speed adrenalin rushes, clinging to Rupert on the back of his bike. As I hope she will understand, it was the *confit* that drove me to it.

On Sundays, the most indulgent of all the days in the Paris week, we criss-crossed the city with a variety of pretexts to distract us from the fantasy of *confit* that lured us on. So we pretended to locate Samuel Beckett's flat near the seriously forbidding Santé prison, gazed laconically at antique markets, listened to the musicians at the Mouffetard market, but it was the prospect of *confit* that weighed with us. We thought we'd found it at lunch after the Mouffetard market in the Place Contrescarpe, but were no longer sure after sampling *Les Fontaines* looking out on the Pantheon. Ah, the elusive search for perfection! I am relieved to say that with the *confit* it is a never-ending quest.

Smashed Duck

This is a version of the dish famously known as Szechuan crispy fried duck. I call it Smashed Duck for reasons which will become apparent. I became an addict – and it does have addictive compulsion – in the seventies in London where we used to repair to The Golden Duck in Hollywood Road as often as our pockets afforded us. It was such a rare and exotic treat, expensive, but worth it for every exquisite morsel, the sensation of which remained with us for days. We could never resist ordering the whole duck between two of us, and would happily not have eaten all day, all week if necessary, to make sure we were sufficiently ravenous.

The dish was presented with a strong sense of theatre. The duck was borne to the table looking, at that point, like any other unassuming dead duck. Then the waiter did his trick. He appeared only to wave his hands over the duck in movements reminiscent of the kung fu movies of the time. There must in fact have been subtle chopping motions, for, before our astonished and admiring gaze, the duck would disintegrate, fall apart into succulent morsels. Smashed duck.

Far from Hollywood Road (the restaurant no longer exists), and even though the dish has become fairly well known, I determined to compensate my cravings and mug up a simple version for myself. It gets me through many an occidental night.

This magnificent duck is served with wafer-thin pancakes, that is part of its magic. Gobbets of smashed duck are scooped up and crammed into the pancakes. They slip down the gullet like torpedoes of bliss.

There are laborious methods for making this supreme dish, as tortuous as only the Chinese could devise. You really need not bother with the rigmarole of pumping air between the skin and flesh with a creaking bicycle pump. Although in deference to Adam who served the best I've ever tasted, perhaps the traditional method, which relies on the direction of the wind, the temperature, the bicycle pump, and other barely speakable rites, may well be worth the anguished nights.

For the less industrious, then, to prepare the duck, cut away the fat and puncture the skin so that excess fat can escape. Pummel star anise, fennel and cumin seeds with Five Spice powder. Rub this mixture vigorously inside the duck and over the skin. Stuff ginger and salt into the cavity. Smear sesame oil over the bird, and bung it in the oven, on a tray so that fat drips clear, and roast until crispy.

The tiresome procedure is making the pancakes, but it is compensated for by the beauty of their thinness and the ingenuity of the method. Fred is a master of the craft.

Pour two thirds of a cup of boiling water into a generous cup of cake flour in a bowl, and mix until combined. Then squidge the mixture in your hands until smooth. Roll it into a ball and leave it to stand for half an hour or so. Lightly flour a working surface and roll out the ball into a fat sausage. Cut it into ten pieces, each about an inch long.

Now the tricky bit. Cut each piece in half and roll each between your palms into a smooth marble. Next with a rolling pin, roll out each of these marbles into a circular shape the diameter of your finger. Paint one with sesame oil, and put another on top. Gently roll out until it almost doubles its size. It is now paper thin. Lay it on a hottish frying pan with nothing added. Flip after a minute as it browns lightly, and do the other side. When you remove it from the pan, it miraculously separates into two perfect wafer-thin pancakes. Repeat the process for the rest of them. You will find that as one cooks, you can roll out the next, and the process dovetails.

Smash the duck when it comes to the table. Practise the mysterious kung fu motions, but you will find you will have to take a knife to it. Slivers of duck are slapped into the pancakes, which are coated with Chinese Hoisin sauce (plum, garlic, chilli, sesame seed and Chinese secrets), adorned with wafers of cucumber and spring onion. Take a fast track to Szechuan, via Fukien if you can.

A Birthday at Aphrodisias

Not all birthdays are good, and of course they get worse with age. Nevertheless, I have a perverse romantic yearning to make them memorable. I couldn't give a

A birthday at Aphrodisias

damn about conventional celebrations – New Year, Christmas etc – for who wants to celebrate with the rest of the world? One craves one's own special significance, and the more ritualised the more memorable. I feel a pang of sorrow for poor Oonagh whose birthday is on New Year's Eve. She consoles herself by assuming the world celebrates with her, which for me would make it all the more depressing.

One criterion of course is the birthday meal, usually dinner (although I must say I have had splendid breakfasts). It is not only, as always, a matter merely or centrally of the food; the place, company and atmosphere are what one remembers most. Sometimes the memory has nothing to do with food at all. If one is abroad, as I have perhaps most often been, one's appetite for speciality is particularly aroused, although it can also prove unpredictable. In Madrid, as I put the suitcase into the boot of the car, I turned to retrieve my jacket slung over the roof, only to find it in that split second gone, not a thief in sight. In the pocket (luckily not the car keys), my passport. So I spent my birthday in the gloomy charge office of a Madrid police station, where everyone kept their eyes downcast and looked miserable. Unable to get to Toledo that day (where we had the birthday prospect of a feast in the Parador), we almost made up for the disappointment with a late night *calamari in umido*, rich, black and decadent.

This time, my romantic spirit was heightened at the prospect of a birthday at Aphrodisias in Turkey, temple of the goddess herself, indeed someone worth sharing the occasion with. As it was the middle of winter it had to be lunch. Even then, dusk would be falling, but that of course would only enhance the romance of the occasion.

So off we set, taking a bus from Pammukale, where we were staying, into the unknown realm of the gods. There was nowhere to stay at Aphrodisias; indeed, there is nothing in the frozen wastelands except the ruins of the temple. That has an extraordinary poignancy and resonance, and gives the journey its significance. Sitting on the ancient stones in the translucent light, we ate a simple picnic to the gods: aubergine with feta, vine leaves with pine nuts and raisins, spicy meatballs and mackerel, fat olives, pickles and *ekmek*, the local bread.

The bus trip had taken much longer than expected, a couple of hours, and the day was short. It was with a sense of shock that we realised suddenly, as the light faded and the temperature dropped, how short. Then a horrible thought struck. When was the next bus back to Pammukale? For some odd reason we hadn't thought this out in advance. Perhaps we had come from somewhere where buses run regularly. As darkness descended, our plight became nasty. There was snow on the mountains and ice on the ground; no shelter except the stones of Aphrodite's cold heart. We looked plaintively at each other, then at the road. We hadn't seen a single vehicle all day.

Out of the frozen blue, suddenly, salvation. Or so it appeared. A coach whooshed alongside, and out spilled fifty gibbering Japanese tourists. They scrambled about snapping pictures. We knew we were saved because on the side of the coach was emblazoned PAMMUKALE. Miraculously, they were on their way to exactly where we wanted to be.

It should have been a simple matter. But we were more naive in those days, and we had not had experience of the Japanese. So I was taken aback when, approaching the tour guide with our plight, he hesitated and looked awkward. There were spare seats on the coach. We offered to pay. Finally, no, he said, the Japanese would not allow it. We protested and argued, desperately. We said it would be like condemning us to freezing to death. The guide was not Japanese, and our perilous predicament made him uneasy. He plucked up courage to speak to the leader of the Japanese party. The answer was no. 'You see,' he said apologetically, 'they see you as beggars. It is not the Japanese way.'

Thus we were left stranded in the middle of winter, in the middle of nowhere, in the middle of the night. It made me think then, and subsequent experiences have exacerbated it, of the ghastly heartlessness of those races who feel themselves superior and so ruthlessly aloof that they consider others expendable, vermin. The attitude of the Japanese tourists was not that distinct from the attitude that impelled Yuko Hisho to devour his foreign girlfriend, a gruesome story I will later relate. Those on the bus would merely have had the satisfaction of our frozen fate at one remove.

Our encounter with this ignoble people had a happy ending. We did not freeze to death, and the Turks who rescued us made us think as highly of them as it made us loathe those who had abandoned us. We started walking towards the road. We knew we could not last the night huddled among the stones. As we walked, the mud of the fields crunched with solid ice beneath our feet. We were exhausted by the time we made the road, and it was pitch dark. We turned in the direction from which the bus had brought us that morning, and to which the Japanese tourists had turned without a backward glance.

A wonky light approached, and we hurled ourselves in its path. It was a wreck of a car, and there were about ten people of all ages and sizes crammed inside. Nobody spoke a word of English. What a testament to them for stopping on that desolate road, squeezing together to fit the strangers in, and dropping us at our hotel, refusing categorically the cash we thrust forward. I think, in retrospect, that the most special thing about this birthday was what it taught me of human nature, at both its extremes.

I have taken satisfaction ever since in hastening to give directions to any lost Japanese tourists I can find;

and sending them as elaborately in the wrong direction as possible.

> ## *Cassoulet*
>
> I first had this remarkable dish in a Basque restaurant in Paris, and followed it with my first Brillat-Savarin, the richest of all cheeses. I am surprised I survived, but am humbled with gratitude, since I have gone on to have, and make, many a splendid cassoulet in different parts of the world. The dish, robust and peasant-earthy, profits from the adaptation and addition of local specialities and ingredients. It is a dry stew based on beans, with a variety of meats according to taste and locality.
>
> I assisted my great mate, and collaborator in film, Bruce, in putting together a sumptuous cassoulet for a dinner party at their house in London, where I am always generously welcomed. It is a dish worth doing only for a party, and Bruce and Kate draw a lively and stimulating group of friends, some of whom are also friends of mine. I remember Verne, who I think more or less owns the Bank of England, and Anthony, the laird of Kalk Bay, latterly of Westminster, were there. We spent much of the day scouring town for the right beans, and were surprised how difficult they were to find. The rest of the day was an abandoned and joyous throwing together of the feast. When Bruce and I cook, the kitchen looks, quite deliriously, like a bomb site.
>
> You need dried white haricot beans, which should soak in cold water overnight, or if time is pressing, boil them for a couple of hours, and soak in fresh water. Pork is the main meat ingredient, together with coarse sausage, to which we added leg quarters of duck (chunks of lamb would be an alternative). Take a pork belly and a good wedge of pork rind cut into strips, and parboil for a few minutes. Drain the beans and put them in a pot on top of the stove. Add the pork to the pot. Throw in a couple of leeks and onions, several garlic cloves, bay leaves,

Many a splendid cassoulet, robust and peasant-earthy

cloves and thyme. Cover with water and a splash of wine, and simmer for over an hour. Then take a pork fillet, stuffed with garlic and well salted and peppered, and brown it in olive oil with the duck quarters. Add them to the pot, together with half a dozen ripe tomatoes, roughly cut, and a couple of diced onions, more garlic and herbs, and the sausages. Cook slowly for an hour.

For the final stage of the cooking, remove the meats, beans, and liquid from the pot. Carve the meats and place them in layers with the beans and liquid in a baking dish in a medium oven for an hour or so, beans forming the bottom and top layers. Sprinkle bread crumbs on top. The dish derives its name from the *cassole* earthenware dish, and is served from it.

Le Grand Vefour

We are showing titbits of Paris to Ivor – *mon oncle sudafricain!* – and have landed up in the street of most sex shops. It is the end of a weary Saturday of traipsing and ogling, and even we are insusceptible to the allures of flesh trembling in every doorway and dark passage. We want the kind we can eat, as a respite from the *life shows* (as the French endearingly advertise) and unsavoury diet of bloated tarts on the rue St Denis, average age eighty.

We stumble into the glorious Palais Royal. There is a dim light at the far corner. We make for it. It is drizzling. It is late, and we are jaded and exhausted. Something simple perhaps . . . just to cheer us up. It is important to see what we looked like. Our jeans are soiled, our T-shirts sweaty, our takkies seared with the dogshit that makes every street in Paris a *foefie* slide to be taken seriously. We are past caring. It looks like a restaurant, although, surprising for Paris, we don't see a menu in the window. We try pressing our shiny noses to the window, but curtains are discreetly drawn. Ivor looks disappointed (he has a keen appetite), raises an eyebrow, shrugs, and pushes open the door.

The instant we enter, we know we have made a major mistake. The shudder runs through the three of us like an electric shock, and we all turn simultaneously to flee back into the gutter from which we have crawled. We have quite evidently entered the drawing room of Louis XVI. The sumptuousness and finery is overwhelming. The air of perfume and fine food wafts towards us. We are terrified by the aghast expression in the eyes of the maitre d', who looks like Bonaparte in full Emperor regalia. Fortunately, we are trapped in a vestibule adjacent to the restaurant, so are spared the shame of other patrons' disdain, the withering contempt of the waiters.

'Excusez-nous,' I stammer, 'nous avons un problème.' (Extraordinary how that word 'problem' translates into almost any situation.)

Napoleon wasn't taken in for a moment. By my French, in the first instance. Hardly raising the temperature of his features (deep chill), he said, it must be conceded, with admirable aplomb, 'For every problem, we have a solution.'

We stared, loose-mouthed. Did he mean *la guillotine*? (We felt we deserved it.)

He whisked us aside, and with a deft touch, dusted us off, squirted us with cologne, knotted silk ties round our necks, and slipped what could only have been St Laurent jackets over our shoulders. Without a trace of embarrassment (he must have been mortified), he threw back the curtains and marched us to a vacant table, as if we were walking on to a yacht (our own). Nobody looked up from their delectable plates, and intimidatingly formal waiters bowed impeccably. We had arrived.

We really did not know how lucky we were. For we quickly discovered, on presentation of the glorious menu (itself a major work of art), that we were in Le Grand Vefour, which is the oldest, indeed first, restaurant in Paris (and perhaps the Western world), established before the Revolution when the Palais Royal was precisely that, a Royal palace, home to the Duc d'Orleans, cousin of the king and a leading conspirator in the Revolution. The overthrow of the ancient regime was plotted where we sat. We felt our gullets contract.

The meal, ah the meal. Was it real? Was it food? This is the very mystique that accords a handful of restaurants in the world the fabled Michelin three stars. It is in its very nature an indefinable sense of exclusivity. Ivor characteristically rose to the occasion, and (with his gold cards in support) we made the most of the wondrous offerings. We hardly knew what we were eating, nothing tasted like food we had ever eaten before. It did not even look like food, unless of a kind presented to the gods. We had never felt happier or more indulged. It is something to do once in your life, even if you have to rob a bank. And don't bother to dress, they do it for you.

We ate like lords of the earth, perhaps even like dukes of Orleans. Artichokes stuffed with foie gras, lamb encrusted in a pastry of vanilla and nuts, pigeon ennobled for Prince Rainier, duck as pink as flamingo feather, caramelised ice cream like a sweet breath of paradise, cheeses suppurating decadence. Was it *les ravioles de foie gras à l'émulsion de crème truffée* that sent us straight to heaven? It hardly seemed to matter, we were quite beyond words.

At the end of this feast, as we fell back in stunned satiety, Ivor told the maitre d' how much we'd enjoyed everything, and could we come back tomorrow. With absolutely no trace of any reflection on ourselves, such that we truly believed it wasn't, he replied with grave regret that the restaurant was fully booked six months ahead. The only reason we had got in was that a rare cancellation had come through minutes before. He didn't go on to say that he'd taken pity on us, but perhaps he had.

Foie Gras

This is perhaps the ultimate indulgence, and one that arouses strong antipathies in some quarters. This is because of the traditional method of production, in which the goose is force-fed until its engorged liver bursts. Some consider this a barbaric indignity. No doubt it is not a pleasant experience for the wretched goose, although it is a sacrifice that gives great pleasure to the fortunate recipients. I am not sure that being throttled, decapitated or hooked in the gullet, are not equally unpleasant means of despatch. That the squeamish should keep clear of the abattoir, is as prudent as keeping out of the kitchen if you can't stand the heat.

It is worth suppressing any conflicting instincts to savour the unique wonder of foie gras. It is of a purity and radiance that is as impossible to catch as sunlight. To feel it in your hands is the most sensual approach to heaven. To cook it takes seconds, but the sensation lingers for what seems close to eternity.

With care and tenderness snip off the vein of skin from the raw liver (use a Laguiole knife if you can). Sprinkle with a little Maldon and black pepper, and lay it reverently in a hot pan. The fat will gush out – it is not a perfect dish for the cholesterol-challenged – and you will need to flip it over once or twice, turning the heat down. It needs to take colour and be gently agitated right through by the heat, the centre should be barely reached. On no account overcook, it is the delicacy of flavour and texture that is supreme. Remove from the pan, and to the juices add a splash of fine dessert wine (Chateau d'Yquem would be perfect), or the glorious fortified aperitif Pineau des Charentes, and a scattering of sweet peeled and pipped grapes. Serve with thin toast, and relish every morsel, as if it were your last meal on earth.

> ### Artichoke Hearts with Shrimps, Mushrooms & Parmesan
>
> It can be laborious to struggle through a whole artichoke, and sometimes it is desirable to go straight for the heart, and leave the leaves for more energetic days. It can also be cruel to observe the uninitiated struggle with an artichoke for the first time, rather like watching a puppy attack a hedgehog.
>
> Select artichokes with big bottoms, for that is where the heart lies. Cook them in salted boiling water until the outer leaves drop off. Strip away the leaves (you will no doubt nibble as you go, dipping them into hot butter), and scrape the hairy chokes from the hearts. This is a starter, so one or two hearts per person will do.
>
> Fry up the mushrooms in olive oil, and add shrimps, garlic and grated parmesan. Put in a dash of crème fraiche to amalgamate. Spoon the mixture over each heart, and decorate with fine-chopped parsley and fresh parmesan.

Magic Mushrooms at the Pampoenpaleis

While the restaurant was under construction, we lived in the labourer's cottage at the edge of the property near the river. We moved Jack, the gardener, and his family into the main house, which the two old boys from whom we'd bought the property had vacated. We called the cottage the *Pampoenpaleis*, and stuck some pumpkins on the tin roof to prove it.

Jack couldn't believe his luck. The decrepit labourer's cottage could not have been a further cry from a palace; it was more or less a ruin. For an unaccountable reason, which I find difficult to justify these days, it held a kind of mad romantic appeal for us, and we felt the main house rather boring. Jack was delighted. At least the house had a proper roof and ceiling and windows; it had electricity and a kitchen. The cottage was falling to

An element of romantic madness set us aglow

pieces; two bare stone rooms with no adornment nor built-in facilities, a primitive outside loo, no bath or shower, and no electricity. We lit paraffin lamps and the coal stove belched black fumes. We had to pump water from the river, and it was ice cold. We joined the local gym so that we could have hot showers. When we visited friends we were overwhelmed with the luxury of turning on a light.

Jack, cosily ensconced in the house, electric heaters and fridges buzzing, lights and television blazing, did not pretend to understand our bizarre choice.

'*Dis mos die nuwe Suid-Afrika,*' he shrugged philosophically.

Sometimes we would challenge friends by inviting them to supper. It was a kind of test. It must have been an adventure for them, and daunting. Abandoning the familiar luxuries of civilised living, they sallied bravely forth into the darkness. At a certain point on the deserted country road they veered into the bush, searching for the flicker of lamps, and entered the gloom of our spartan hut. We had to ply them with a great number of drinks. They were always polite, indeed unremittingly flattering, but there was always a flicker of relief as they set off for the comforts of home.

It must have had something to do with the food we produced, unbelievably all done on the ghastly old Dover stove with one burner. This was the beginning of the great One Pot cooking experience. I was driven to it by desperation and necessity. It amazes me to recall the feasts we threw together, and the raucous merriment they occasioned. Friends returned time and again, so it couldn't have been that bad.

One rain-sodden autumn night was not untypical. I had collected pine ring mushrooms and ceps in the forest, and planned a simple wild mushroom pasta together with a pot-roast chicken stuffed with more mushrooms, doused in crème fraiche and coriander. One of our friends, wearing a kaftan, had gone to the main house by mistake, and was led to us by Jack, shaking his head and muttering, '*Kyk, die man dra 'n rok.*' This was about as decadent as you could get in the woods outside Franschhoek.

As we settled amid guttering candles and lamps, glowing Ndebele blankets and drapes on the walls, Noria Mabasa's sculptures looming in the shadows, there was a hollow knock at the door. Appreciate that the hut is in the middle of the bush, no lights, no neighbours, at that stage no dog. (That was why later we got the noble Sam, the Alsatian with a Rottweiler's backside, a grin from ear to ear, but a fine set of teeth: our protector and salvation.) Silence fell, and some of the party looked anxious, suddenly very aware of our vulnerability.

I went to the door and opened it on to a pitch-dark howling storm. Two battered men swayed into view. I was gruff, masking my fear, but they appeared as taken aback at my appearance as I was at theirs. As I deciphered what they were saying in voices slurred with alcohol, it was plain why. The hut had once operated as a shebeen and they were after drink. They expected a woman called Beauty and could not work out what I was doing there. It would take too long to explain.

The frisson made everyone the more ebullient. In attempting to flambé the chicken, precarious on the stove, I almost set the hut alight. Flames leapt up the walls and seared the ceiling. It seemed part of the show. Friends tucked into the pasta and chubby with gusto. An element of romantic madness set us aglow, and the conversation flowed like wine. There was a sinister pause when I chaffed them, with a straight face, that I had of course sliced one *Amanita phalloides* (the Death Cap) into the mixture, so that the meal was like Russian roulette. Little consolation was taken by my assurance that by the time the symptoms appeared it would be too late to do anything about it. Just as faces fell, they saw the glint in my eye and laughter was restored. I remember Marilyn staggering off into the night, swearing it was the best meal of her life. Perhaps she got the magic mushroom.

Chubby with Wild Mushrooms

The first rains of autumn bring out the mushrooms in the forest, and the hidden mushroomer in oneself. It is a glorious opportunity to haul out the wellies and slush about under the pine trees.

My family is quite paranoid about mushrooms, which my mother endearingly called toadstools. Her father, my grandfather, fed me one under the pear tree when I was a child, for reasons that have never been perfectly clarified, and I was rushed to hospital to have my stomach pumped. Years later my sister did the same when her Labrador chomped one. So it is perhaps surprising that I have a renegade passion for mushrooming, and slapping the spoils into a variety of dishes. My family bravely nibbles at a corner, and spits it out.

Not that one should be too cavalier. There are one or two mushrooms that will make you very ill and perhaps kill you, but it is more common to be struck by lightning. The famous last words of the mushroom victim are, 'Never had such a delicious meal in my, uh, life'. So there are compensations even there.

The simple rule for absolute safety is never touch a mushroom that has white gills. They look deadly. The two most readily identifiable, one hundred per cent safe varieties are the pine ring and the *cèpes* (to the French) or *porcini* (to the Italians), the incomparable *Boletus edulis*. This is the most highly prized mushroom in Europe (we don't even think of the truffle) and, with its spongiform underside and swollen stem, it springs out of the earth to declare itself. Peel away the top skin and any slime. The lesser boletuses are horribly slimy and not worth eating. The pine ring is more common, and once you have seen and sniffed the sweet sensuous aroma of one you will never mistake it. The test is to cut the stem in half which will reveal the livid orange ring from which it gets its name.

Pick them fresh, as they emerge from their subterranean hibernation, a day after rain when the sun stirs them to rise. It is a treasure hunt to savour. Brush traces of earth or pine needle from the surfaces with tissue paper and slice them up. Best to fry them in olive oil, with bacon and garlic, if you like, before adding to any dish.

For the chubby, stuff it with a handful of uncooked mushrooms, salt and pepper, slosh over some olive oil and roast until tender with the skin crackling. The test is to stick a fork into the thigh and see that the juices run clear and not pink. Then pour over the mushrooms cooked with bacon into which you have stirred a good punnet of crème fraiche. Chubby is redolent of the fragrant autumn woods.

Babette's Feast

Whenever I make lists of the best films I have seen, they always have a rather quirky diversity. And of course they change. Some stalwarts that often appear are *Last Tango in Paris, Paris Texas, Death in Venice, The American Friend, Aguirre: the Wrath of God, The Passenger, The Pillow Book, Cries and Whispers, The Colour of Paradise, Les Enfants du Paradis, Casablanca.* The one that always appears is *Babette's Feast*, the classic of culinary movies, based on the story by Karen Blixen.

It is not only a superbly sensitive rendition of the tale, it is a feast that moves beyond the stimulation of taste to reach enduring spiritual and emotional depths. It is a paradigm of my sense of the integration and synthesis of food with essential qualities of life. Babette, in striving to overcome barriers and unite divergencies, becomes in the achievement of her feast the true artist, for whom the creative act confers meaning and satisfaction.

'It is terrible and unbearable to an artist . . . to be

encouraged to do, to be applauded for doing, second best. Through all the world goes the long cry, from the heart of the artist: Give me leave to do my utmost!'

For his sixtieth birthday, my father-in-law commandeered a restaurant to replicate Babette's Feast in every detail. It could not have been a finer commemoration. I preserve the memory in the invitation (more like notes to a concert: indeed the meal was a symphony), which brings juices to my lips as I read it now.

We started with delectable little canapés to amuse the mouth, as the French say *(amuse-gueule)*. This is invariably the sign that a great meal lies ahead. The soup was mock turtle. Delicate Russian blinis with caviar followed. Then a *mousseline* of crayfish, tantalising the tastebuds with the sex of the sea. Sorbets to clear the palate before the climax, the theatrical presentation of quail *en croute* (or as Babette has it, *en sarcophage*, literally in a coffin of pastry). It is a dish that brings a gasp to the lips. The heads of the little birds are propped into place as a garnish, upsetting (I was delighted to see) some of the more queasy of the guests, who, in surreptitiously pushing the heads to the sides of their platters, allowed me to snatch them away. I must have crunched about fifteen with alacrity.

We had cheeses and pudding (rum baba, allowing the chef a different opportunity to show off his superb touch with pastry), meticulously selected wines from France, cognac and liqueurs ... the night of celebration passed in a voluptuous trance of bonhomie and good fellowship. But it was the quail – indeed the heads – that I carried away most intimately in my memory.

Quail with Hanepoot Grapes

One of the few sensations I miss about Franschhoek is the harvesting of the grapes in the autumn. The essentially

Provençal character of the village is restored, all too briefly, as the wagons, bursting with fresh shining grapes, trundle towards the presses, drawn by slow tractors. For this recipe, you need to get to the grapes before the vintners do. Best are the first sweet hanepoots of the season, tasting of sugar and sunshine.

Braise the quails, duly sprinkled in pepper and Maldon, in olive oil until golden. Add a splash of brandy, then a glass of white wine (Hanepoot by preference), and simmer gently with a good chicken stock. As with all birds, the cooking must never be harsh. Blanch the grapes separately in hot water and peel them.

When the doughty little quails are done, remove them and thicken the juices with a blob of butter and flour. Stir to a good consistency. Toss the quails back in and add the grapes to simmer for a few minutes. Arranged concentrically on a platter, the dish looks, and tastes, green and golden and lovely, like a poem by Dylan Thomas.

Roast Quail Piero

Marinade quails in a tight bowl with a few sage leaves, a bay leaf, diced onion, pepper and salt, and white wine. Reserve the marinade, the aroma of which is delicious. Brown the birds in butter. Add a dash of brandy and flambé. Add the strained marinade and cook in the oven for about forty-five minutes. Remove the birds, and make a sauce from the juices and flour, adding cream, chopped capers and Dijon mustard.

Quail with Spices

Truth to tell, you can do as you wish with quail, just as you can with chicken. They are marvellously versatile, the soft flesh absorbing different flavours with ease, and should be put to the test.

This time simmer them gently in a mixture of spices. Grind the whole spices, cardamom, cumin, coriander (always better

> freshly ground rather than bought precrushed, where they lose intensity and look all too much like ashes). Rub vigorously into the flesh and crevices of the birds. Braise in olive oil, turn the heat low and simmer in a little water, topping up as you go along. When they are done, remove and add to the pan cream and fresh coriander to toss over the quail. You could have chilli in the cooking to taste.
>
> Roasted peppers chime well with the exotic spiciness of the taste. Serve with couscous or Basmati rice. A good variant in spices is Chinese Five Spice with ginger and nutmeg. Spice up your imagination.

As Good As It Gets

At school, I picked out three of my friends who were made for success, and I was right. Niels was usually at the top of the list, and I immortalised him among those interminable comparatives that were the bane of Afrikaans lessons: *so rooi soos bloed, so wit soos sneeu* ... He was *so goed soos Niels*, abbreviated later simply to *so goed soos*. So we would say, *So Goed Soos* is coming to dinner tonight, and everyone knew who it was.

Actually Niels was the first among us who could actually cook, and did. We were still in the thrall of mothers and Lizzy Rapoos – occasionally a pizza at the place around the corner – and the prospect of boiling an egg or putting a chicken in the oven was beyond us. We assumed too much, or perhaps thought it all a kind of miracle. The best I could do was a peanut butter sandwich, although I must admit that I preferred Fred to make it for me, and often – I'm rather chagrined to remember – actually woke her in the dead of night when I returned from a party – or 'hop' as we used to say – dragged her comatose from her bed, and had her make me a sarmie, with a glass of cold milk. In some ways I must have been a model elder brother.

Niels cooked sirloin *medium rare*, knew the secret of making chips crisp, by frying them twice (he even called them *frites*), and made a mean Béarnaise sauce. No wonder we thought him a genius. He persists in later life with a love and flair for cooking, and does not bat an eyelid at rustling up a dinner for ten or twenty on many nights around his farmhouse table. Should he hesitate or falter, which of course would be quite unlike him, Carey is always at hand to scream, 'Oh for God's sake, get on with it!'

So Carey's birthday party was taken seriously. So Goed Soos actually banged together a banquet table that could seat fifty. He made spectacular flaring lamps and a throne for Carey to preside from. And – with nonchalance – he tossed together dinner for fifty. Sirloin Béarnaise, of course.

I was to make a speech, and for some reason was tempted to make a bit of an arse of myself. I arrived suitably dickied up in black tie as the occasion demanded, but added gaudy plastic earrings that were meant to look like rubies, and smeared lipstick and eyeshadow on my face. My hair was in a velvet bow, something I usually detest on middle-aged balding men, pathetically trying to pull the young girls. What was I thinking? Perhaps that it might amuse Carey, who has a deliciously wicked sense of the ridiculous; perhaps a temptation to shock, ever so mildly, what I took to be the conservative men's men of White River.

The trouble was that by the time I got to the party I was already having second thoughts, the main thought being what a tit I looked. So I crept in the back way to Carey's boudoir where she was putting final touches to her ensemble. She threw her arms around me and shrieked with laughter, so I was fortified and, on her arm, made a grand entrance.

Everyone was assembled, and at first glance, it did look a rather predictable country affair with all the men huddled on one side of the room, and their wives fluttering about on the other. It was made worse that I hardly knew anyone there. As I entered on Carey's arm, a hush fell and all eyes stared at the apparition. I was overwhelmed with the realisation that what they were all thinking was, *Who's that ghastly poof that poor Carey's holding up?*

My eyes flickered from the bunch of boys – they looked very macho and seemed to meanly slit their eyes back at me – to the gaggle of girls, all of whom looked ravishing. I realised at once where my audience lay, but took a diversion via Niels's mother on the sofa in the centre of the room. She held a glass of champagne and glittered with jewels and earrings that were real. So I settled myself at her side, helped myself to the magnum, and gossiped away about ladies' things. This was an effective strategy. The boys relaxed and returned to their scrum, and I felt the girls looking at me as a sweetie who devoted kind attention to Niels's mother.

As soon as I wrenched myself away from comparing earrings with Niels's mother, and made for the wives, the slit eyes of the husbands struck me like radar. I felt I had to break the tension. It was then or never. So I strode straight into the lions' den, made directly for the most macho of all the boys, and gave him a smacking kiss on the cheek. There was a moment of suspense, perhaps horror. Then Richard, to his great credit, clasped me warmly and yelled with laughter. The tension was broken and I was part of the party. It was a grand success.

Sirloin with Rocket

It was not that long ago that we first tasted rocket in the Cape. It came from the progressive Dutch chef who had the Chez Michel restaurant in Somerset West. The taste of such a herb came as a revelation. It is now almost as common as lettuce, but the bitter tang is still as distinct.

Rocket is shown to best advantage in this refreshingly light, simple dish. I relished it in the village *ristorante* outside Lucca as a prenuptial feast before Giles and Vanessa's wedding.

Splash the sirloin with olive oil and balsamic vinegar, and spatter with Maldon and black pepper. Smear Dijon or French wholegrain mustard over the top. Roast the sirloin whole. When still rare, remove and delicately slice over a generous platter of rocket, doused in olive oil and balsamic.

Northumberland Pudding

In the Fresh Woods household, loyalties are fierce. Peter's mother had roots in Northumberland, mine are in Yorkshire, so occasionally a War of the Roses erupted, it must be said in the most genteel manner. For the purposes of this recipe, it is Northumberland, rather than Yorkshire, Pudding. Yorkshire Pudding was dismissively known at Freshers as 'Dogse Pudding', Peter claiming that as the closest approximation.

As this is a recipe from Freshers, it is one that relies on correct proportions, so here they are. Take a firm baking dish, close to 9 by 11 inches for these proportions. Whisk together two eggs with barely two cups of flour, sifted airily, and add a cup of milk and two thirds of a cup of water. Heat two tablespoons of beef dripping from the joint with which the Pudding is to be served, until it is smoking hot. Pour in the mixture over the heat, and let it regain its heat. Place the dish in a preheated oven at 200 degrees for forty minutes.

You are now qualified to take up the cudgels.

Giles's Last Banquet

My friend Giles is a flamboyant character who – not all at the same time – has two Aston Martins in case one needs a service, can drink a dozen bottles of sake at Mr

Wing's and not fall over, can make a few million and lose it and make it again, refurbishes mansions for Mick Jagger, consorts with gentry and plumbers with equal charm, tells a cabinet minister to get stuffed, laughs and parties until everyone else drops. He is hugely talented and lives a life that the rest of us can only fantasise about. Not surprisingly, when he goes down, he goes down in style.

I have known Giles up and down, mostly up, and am a great admirer of his resilience, energy, and flamboyant, sometimes roguish, charm. He has a talent for falling with his bottom in the butter. He lived in one of the grandest houses in London, certainly the grandest I have known. It was the Mitford mansion in Rutland Gate, where poor Unity shot herself in the mews after rejection by Adolf Hitler, and almost everyone else. The house, five storeys of it, was more like a palace, and Giles had refurbished it with exotic extravagance. In the basement, an Olympic swimming pool; a palatial kitchen on the ground floor, where we consumed scores of wonderful ebullient meals (he is also of course an inspired cook – and, incidentally, someone who relishes bread and gravy as much as I do); a ballroom on the first floor; fifteen or twenty bedrooms, and right at the top, overlooking the Russian Orthodox Church, the suite where I often stayed. Giles was a characteristically generous and vivacious host, and made it seem like home to me.

There was a time it all had to end, at least temporarily. If Giles is down, it is never for long, and, sensing an impending relapse, he elected to make his exit memorable. He invited fifty of his best friends to a banquet in the ballroom. It was lavishly catered, in my recollection there was a butler hovering behind each chair. There was a quartet playing in the drawing room, and a band revving it up through the night. Champagne flowed on silver trays, borne by pretty girls in black aprons. The dinner was exquisite and went on long into the night.

Giles at the villa in Lucca

The rich and famous, the young and the beautiful . . . a Gatsby of a party.

Late, I put an arm round Giles's shoulder. I knew that, for the moment, he was short of cash.

'It was glorious. But who's paying?'

He looked at me with insouciant disdain. Put an arm round my shoulder, more in pity, and confided, as if he were elucidating to an idiot, at least not to one of the rich and famous.

'Don't worry, darling. It'll all be fine.'

It always is.

Giles's Coronation Chubby

This is a classic dish, and like all classics, it is often abused and universalised to the point of cliché. And like all clichés, it is susceptible to revival by a dash of originality and quirky flair. Giles effects such a transformation with ease. It is a dish only worth doing for a party, and Giles often flings it together for twenty guests at Sunday lunch on the lawn at Hambledon House in the glorious Surrey countryside.

Immerse a few fine free-range chubbies in equal parts of white wine, mango juice and cold water, and poach with leeks, onions, carrots, bay leaves and salt.

Dice a couple of onions and sweat in butter and white wine over gentle heat. Take a tin of crushed pineapple, and add its juice (reserve the pulp), and a couple of spoons of mild curry powder.

When chubbies are cooked, remove and allow to cool before removing flesh. Reduce the chicken stock fast over high heat to half its original volume. Add the onion curry mix, and a couple of tins of coconut cream, and continue to reduce down to half its volume again until it is almost glutinous. Allow to cool.

Rustle up a mayonnaise, and combine with half its volume of tomato paste. Add the pineapple pulp previously reserved, generous dollops of apricot jam, some peach chutney, and a few spoons of paprika. Strain the cooled onion curry mix, and spoon it in. Test for flavour. Massage this combined sauce into the chubby chunks, and dust the finished dish with paprika. Serve on rice, to which you might add cardamom cloves, almonds and raisins. It is a most consoling, cool dish for a summer's day.

Breakfast at Leonardo da Vinci's Castle

Not quite, but the castle was sketched by Leonardo, so I feel I can get away with the tantalisation.

The castle is called Il Calcione, and it commands a hillside or two outside Arezzo, as far as the eye can see. I was lucky enough to stay there as a guest some time ago with a girlfriend who was a cousin of the Count. We had driven down to Tuscany from Lake Garda, where I had, as a tribute to Pasolini who had recently been murdered – then run over and squashed so that no bit of him bigger than a postage stamp survived – insisted on stopping at Salo, the town he infamously depicted as a refuge for the Fascist sadists in his notorious last film (loosely based on Sade's work) *The 120 Days of Sodom*. I recall we had a most comforting dish of rabbit stew, and there seemed depressingly few sadists about.

The girlfriend and I were allocated different towers, such was the old-fashioned austerity of the castle and the noble cousins. We had to tiptoe over the flagstones, and talk in whispers. The old aristocrats were formal and intimidating, and meals at the twenty-seater dining table were heavy going (the more so as I couldn't follow a word of the conversation). I concentrated on the food, most of which came directly from the estate to the kitchen. It was thrilling to watch the garrison of faithful retainers rolling out the pasta by hand on long marble top tables in the mornings, thrusting bread into the ovens, plucking birds and pounding meats, sifting salad

In each of us lurks an aristocrat with a grand castle in the Tuscan hills

leaves and herbs, baskets of fruit and vegetables.

Breakfast set the tone. There were fresh cheeses and home-cured hams and sausages, grapes, olives and figs, crusty bread warm from the oven and studded with herbs, sweet pastries. The main dish was a surprise, and arrived on huge platters in front of each of us: a tiny crispy bird, beak and head and feet and all, plucked and rigid, a rather touching sight. Poor Tessa, who was a vegetarian, had to push her plate politely aside, and concentrate on the decadently sticky purple figs. There was a flagon of wine on the table, made from their own grapes and pressed on the estate, which the butler assiduously poured into our glasses. That was impressive for breakfast, and the wine was Keatsian: *cooled a long age in the deep-delved earth, with beaded bubbles winking at the brim, and purple stained mouth.*

It is extraordinary how quickly one acclimatises to an environment such as this. It took only a day or so for me, at least, to believe this my natural state, and to feel resentful that it lasted all too briefly. In all of us lurks an aristocrat with a grand castle in the Tuscan hills, begging to be let out.

Risotto

This is a magical dish. In the category of omelette and soufflé, it has a delicacy and freshness that makes it a supreme thing of its kind. It is deceptively simple, must be perfect, and is utterly rapturous. Success relies on careful attention and perfect timing. Get it wrong and you may as well throw it out of the window.

First essential is the rice. Risotto originates in the north of Italy, and is as famous, as perfect and as proud a tradition as pasta is in the south. The rice is particular and unlike any other in that it is a round hard-centred grain that lends itself to slow cooking. The best is the *superfino* grade from Arborio, and it is worth every euro. Don't be tempted to try the dish with any substitute. There are many cheap and nasty rices about, some of which are adequate for the cuisines they are intended to match, others of which are merely the dreary staples they are. It is an insult to the finesse of risotto to dumb it down with any other rice. It will end up a stodgy mush which your guests will politely decline or toss over their shoulders into the bin.

As with pasta, the principle is simplicity. The true experience is in the taste and texture of the rice itself; it does not need titivation or embellishment. What is important is the stock in which it cooks. So make a jolly good broth from chicken or duck carcass, boiled with carrots, celery, onion and herbs. This is the base of the risotto and is delicious in itself.

Start with a good wedge of butter simmering quietly in the pot. Add a diced onion on a low heat so that it softens but does not brown. Throw in the rice, about a cup a person if it is the full meal. With the wooden spoon toss the rice in the butter so that each grain is coated. Do it delicately and make certain nothing burns or sticks to the pot. When you are satisfied, add the strained stock to cover the rice. Put in a few precious fronds of saffron which will add not only a sensual subtlety of flavour, but the exquisite umber-gold lustre.

It is necessary to keep a beady eye on the risotto throughout the cooking process. This is to monitor the level of fluid and ensure that it does not cook too fast or burn. Slow simmering with the gradual topping up of stock fluid is the secret. It will take about twenty minutes and you will need to test the rice now and then. What you are looking for is the *moment critique* when the texture is firm but not soft to the bite. *Al dente* as the Italians insist: to the tooth, in other words, feel the bite. A moment too soon and the rice is underdone; a moment too late and it has lost the bite. It is a tricky business. Blend in gobbets of butter and generous grated parmesan; do not mangle the rice by vigorous stirring. Be gentle. Remember that each grain is to be savoured.

You might add finely diced zucchini or fresh peas to the cooking as the risotto nears completion. Prawns or slivers of chicken are also acceptable, although the true aficionado prizes the unadorned dish above all. When served, the risotto must be eaten immediately so that the texture, as with a perfect omelette or soufflé, is not lost. It should be only just liquid, neither soup nor thick cream, just perfect.

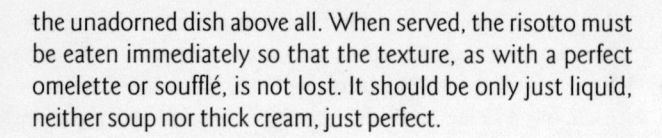

Crab Feast on the Isis

One of the joys of Oxford is the covered market on the High Street, where one finds butchers, fishmongers, greengrocers and purveyors of cheeses, olives and pasta, who are blissfully not supermarket clones, and appear refreshingly Dickensian. The seasonal variations are vividly realised: pheasant, partridge, mushrooms, raspberries, asparagus, oysters and crab come and go with the times of year.

I spent a lot of time in Oxford, on and off, despite being a Cambridge man by education. There is sometimes supposed to be a sense of rivalry between these great institutions, but I think it is mostly in the minds of those who have never been to either. There are many bad jokes, such as, How can you tell an Oxford man from a Cambridge one? An Oxford man rinses his hands after a pee, a Cambridge man before. (Or vice-versa.) I will admit that the annual debates at the combined Old Members get-togethers can be brutal, in the most civilised fashion, of course. In any event, I never considered myself disloyal, and am happy to make the frightful admission that, as a city, and in terms of food and restaurants, Oxford entices me more than Cambridge, where the east wind blows remorselessly off the Urals, and everyone speaks through blocked noses.

At the covered market, we often selected weighty crabs (the ratio of weight to size is critical), and snatched them from their temporary beds of straw. Then plunged them into a boiling pot on the Aga at the Castle on the river, with its idyllic Venetian aspect, under the misty

Never more voluptuously than at the ritual crab feasts

bridge looking over the dark water.

We had fine times at the Castle. Students and friends would gather for evenings of wit and games, the cut and thrust of debate and challenge. We ate and drank famously, never more voluptuously than at the ritual crab feasts. For the eating of crab should be a ritual, undertaken with Dionysian gusto. It is not for the faint-hearted. The claws are smashed open so that shards of shell fly in all directions, and the silky sweet flesh is drawn out, doused in butter and garlic. It is often a prelude to wild debauchery.

David Malouf's gloriously evocative, and erotic, poem *The Crab Feast*, arouses appetite for a love feast. Renditions during such occasions were moments to be savoured.

> *Deep down*
> *I am with you in the dark. The secret flesh of*
> *my tongue enters a claw ...*
>
> *We are one at last. Assembled here*
> *out of earth, water, air*
> *to a love feast.*

The second last of the Piers Gaviston parties was held at the Castle. The society, one of the most famous, or notorious, of the University, commemorated Gaviston who was the lover of Edward the Second, put to death for his affair with the King by having a red hot poker inserted in his rectum. The President of the Society was, with true Oxford sangfroid, called The Poker. Every year a party, celebrated for its decadent and flamboyant style, was held in Oxford, and I attended the penultimate one in the company of young Bismarcks, Spencers, Guinnesses, and a host of Oxford glitterati, most of them unrecognisable in drag. It was the following year that Olivia Channon, daughter of a member of the Cabinet, died of a drug overdose after the party, and the tradition came to a grinding end.

Dim Sum Duck Tongue

I first had Dim Sum one late Sunday morning in London's Chinatown with my friends David and Nica in the mid seventies. In those dark days, Chinese restaurants at home were few, and offered a dismally routine fare of sweet and sour pork plastered in msg. The delicate finesse of bamboo baskets glittering with exotic morsels was thrilling.

'Nothing like a bit of the old chicken foot,' said David with his customary savoir faire, stuffing it whole down his gullet. It amazed me that a chicken foot was just that, in all its sad, calloused tawdriness. It didn't taste quite as repellent as it looked, but I was still drawn to the steamed prawn dumplings in their soft shells.

Over the years, and particularly on visits to London, where Chinatown and the Bayswater Road vie for excellence, I became a devotee of Dim Sum, and savoured every delicacy, however uncongenial it might appear in translation, with relish. There is no more refined way to while away a Sunday morning, with lashings of jasmine tea. The only place to my mind that rivals the famous emporia of London for Dim Sum, is the grandly faded *Le Président* in the Bellville quarter of Paris (so called after a visit by President Mitterand, *le Roi* himself), which, like so many other discoveries in that endlessly fascinating city, make it alone worth the visit.

But, until recently, I had not tasted duck's tongue. I did so on a visit to a famous Chinese emporium in the Bayswater Road with a charming student from Kazakhstan, whom I met in Oxford. She was used to a diet of beetroot and vodka, so was even more taken aback than I by the prospect ahead of us. I wondered what duck tongue would look like. After my initial chicken foot experience, I shouldn't have been surprised. The Chinese are not discreet when it comes to food. If it walks, swims, or crawls, eat it, just as it is.

So duck's tongue, which should be written ducks' tongue, is just that. Blue, once slithery (you can tell), now desiccated, longer than you might imagine. Not an appetising prospect. But the true surprise, indeed mild horror, was in the quantity that squirmed (well, not quite) out of the delicate eggshell bowl. It would be an exaggeration to say hundreds, but that is what it looked like. Duck tongues pullulating in the bowl. It took all my courage as a Dim Summer of strong stomach to stab at the first three or four with a chopstick and ram them (still imagining the squirm) down my throat. After that it was not so bad. The texture is not too unsettling, and duck tongue tastes just like duck tongue. Soy sauce might help the queasy.

The experience did nothing to dispel my admiration for the cuisine, although I might not have the need to try this particular morsel in the near future. Well, perhaps with a young student from Kazakhstan.

Summer in Provence

Linda and I arrived to take up residence at our *mas*, or fortified medieval farmhouse, in Vaison la Romaine in the Vaucluse, in Provence, at a most inauspicious moment. The town was reeling from the worst flood disaster in its long history – and the greatest natural disaster in the country in living memory – in which over a hundred people had been swept away, and as many houses reduced to matchsticks. There had been a rumble in the mountains on a clear day, and, with paralysing suddenness, a maelstrom overwhelmed the town. A wall

Enchanted days roaming the markets

of water thirty metres high burst upon the town, tearing houses to shreds and reducing vehicles to spaghetti. It swelled the usually placid river which meandered through the town centre to a rampaging serpent. Houses were literally sheared in two, bridges splintered, as the flood, carrying the shredded carcasses of cars and caravans from the camping site in the mountains on its crest, struck with full force the Roman bridge at the epicentre of the town.

The bridge groaned, and held. It was all that was left of the town centre, a lone heroic beacon, as the waters subsided: a glowing tribute to history and the engineering acumen of the Roman founders.

Our arrival passed unnoticed, or more unnoticed than it would anyway have been, as the town swung into emergency recovery. Foreigners were less welcome than usual, and we were hardly accorded a passing glance. Perhaps, if we were noticed at all, we might be seen as scapegoats for the tragedy, so we were relieved that our *mas* was on the outskirts of town, sturdy as a rock with walls ten foot thick, and sufficiently elevated to have escaped the flood.

As the summer settled, and memory of the disaster faded, Peter and Barbara came to stay. We had an idyllic, enchanted few days, roaming the markets – one in each neighbouring town or village every day – tasting olives and olive oils in nearby Nyons, the olive capital of France, and returning to gargantuan feasts, lunches in the courtyard or next to the deep blue pool, dinners around the long kitchen table among the cobwebs, heavy beams and old stones. We ate plump duck breasts and decadent duck *confits*, fresh salmon over the open fire, *coquilles* St Jacques melting on the tongue, succulent *gigots* of lamb smothered in wild herbs that thrust up along the footpaths, vivid cheeses, tapenades, pâtés and breads. Peter was astonished at my ability to assume a Gallic shrug and emit a gurgling susurration in my throat, which the market vendors affected to understand. As I gesticulated and went 'Aaargh', they would helpfully fill in a word, which I gratefully confirmed.

To walk off our indulgent feasts, we strode the forests and mountain paths, grasping handfuls of thyme and rosemary, seeing a bee orchid in bloom, and catching a glimpse of a golden snake darting into the foliage. *Attention, le viper!* We drove up Mont Ventoux, the highest peak in Provence, and felt dizzy at the vertical distress. Worse, as Peter remarked, was the rapid sensation of ageing in the landscape itself, as clematis, roses and spruces gave way, in seconds, to the relentless tundra. We felt like dogs whose lives speed up towards the end. Finally, and most rapturously, we tore off our clothes and plunged naked into the icy depths of the Fontaine de Vaucluse, where Petrarch romped so deliriously with Laura. The Japanese tourists, gawking and stabbing the air with cameras, had never seen the like of it.

Tricolore Salmon

I name this dish after the flag of France, the three colours. Here, with salmon, the colours are scorched pink, dark pink, and fresh salmon pink. Pink is not a colour, generally, that I like, and it is not the right word perhaps for salmon, as it is not for flamingo. Whatever the colour of salmon is, it is rapturous. Pink, as a word, will have to do; the real sensation of the colour, like the sky at dawn, defies definition.

I first tasted this way of cooking salmon at a restaurant in Antwerp. The standard of food in Belgium is very high, and very expensive. It is one of the things that this prosperous and self-satisfied nation do well, together with lace and sublime chocolate. I never saw a single beggar in Belgium over the years I lived there.

It is regrettable that fresh salmon does not occur in the

Whatever the colour of salmon, it is rapturous

southern hemisphere, one is compelled to use the 'fresh frozen' Norwegian import, or try it with salmon trout, where the fillets tend to be measly by comparison. Do not hesitate to get friends coming from Europe to bring you a whole fresh salmon. Should it be Scottish, allow them to stay for ever. What is required is a good fat fillet, deboned and shimmering with that indescribable salmon iridescence. The market at Vaison never disappointed. Mae and Theuns cooked it over the cavernous open fire at our *mas* on freezing winter nights, when the snow backed high against the stone walls and the logs burnt low. They claim its delicious nourishment got them through the winter, and tempted them to snuggle closer in bed. We did it in spring, summer, and autumn too.

Slap the whole fillet into a sizzling pan lightly buttered or splashed with olive oil. Let it scorch and permeate, but not burn, the outer layer, turning it over so that both sides take colour. Then turn down the heat and watch carefully. Imagine the fillet in three layers. What you are trying to achieve is the scorching of the outer layer so it is cooked through, then the light braising of the second layer so it is barely cooked, then the pristine rawness of the central innermost layer. *Voilà le Tricolore!*

To prepare the salmon, be as minimalistic as possible. As with all supremely delicate things, there is no need to add anything to what is naturally superlative. A dash of lemon juice, black pepper and Maldon if you like; do not pollute further. When the desired three-coloured effect is realised and the salmon resembles a Swiss Roll (it is a rapid process, no fish should be cooked for long), whip out the salmon and deftly toss crème fraiche into the juices. Whisk to a sauce and toss over the salmon. Add a sprig of fennel if you are trying to be a classic cook. Fennel is an excellent accompanying vegetable, braised or baked whole, and crisp to the bite.

Stuffed Calamari

Calamari has taken time to come into its own, as something worth eating and not simply bait. My friend Billy would refuse to eat it, nor allow anyone else to order it in his party. To him, remembering the war in Italy, it was as depressing as pizza. The same was thought of crayfish until quite recently. My mother remembered her brothers buying it for sixpence at the side of the road, and baiting their hooks.

These days, it is becoming something of a delicacy (not yet as astronomic as crayfish), particularly when young and innocent. Clean the whole calamari, reserving the ink and tossing away the hard and nasty bits. Separate the tube from the feelers and purple tendrils, and beat with a mallet to tenderise. There is nothing as revolting as chewy, tough calamari.

Cook up spinach, mushrooms, and shrimps. The spinach you will have to drain, as it is mostly water, the mushrooms are ready when the water in them has evaporated and the pan is dry, and the shrimps you swirl in olive oil and garlic. Mash the spinach and add nutmeg, cut up the mushrooms and combine with the shrimps. Add condiments to taste. Stuff the mixture into the calamari tubes, securing the ends with a skewer. Then fry the tubes lightly in a little olive oil, to which add the feelers and tendrils with some garlic. When the tubes have taken colour, add the ink from the calamari, which will stain them deep purple.

Seared Tuna

Fresh tuna is dark vulva-red, the colour of blood and sensuality. It represents the point at which fish becomes flesh. It bears no relation at all to the nasty grey stuff that comes in tins, which impecunious students throw miserably over their spaghetti.

Cut the fresh flesh-dark tuna into long fillets. Marinade in equal parts of sesame and soya oil, to which add splashes of olive oil, sherry and lemon juice, and suggestions of honey, ginger, garlic, diced chives, and Chinese Five Spice powder as highlights.

Toss the steaks on to the hottest griddle, and momentarily

The pilgrimage to Lacoste

sear the edges. Remove and slice into bite-size morsels. Serve with crisp French fries and a salad.

In the Shadow of the Marquis

I remarked nonchalantly to some passing guru, 'I read nothing but the Marquis de Sade'. Her eyes popped. 'My God, you *are* the Marquis!' So much for passing gurus.

The legacy of Sade, the most brilliant thinker of his age, lives on in the ruins of his castles around Provence. I have traced the pilgrimage, and time and again I return to Lacoste, the most austere of the surviving citadels. There is a simple inn below the chateau where the *patron* looks as dissipated as Sade would have liked to look, and his beautiful daughter on her bicycle is a Justine turning to Juliette.

In one of my sojourns in Sade country, I got to know the owner of the Chateau of Lacoste, a humble villlage schoolmaster with a glint in his eye. André had grown up in the shadow of the Marquis's ruined chateau, which he felt hanging over him like a sword, and had always felt it deserved something better, that the spirit trapped in the ruins was yearning for release. So he saved his francs, laboriously contacted all the surviving relatives, and gradually bought the chateau that he planned to restore to its original sombre glory, stone by stone. He knew it would take several lifetimes, but he was proud to begin. He liked the thought that someone engaged in future restoration could say, 'My grandfather worked here.'

Sometimes, hammering away late at night, he would be accosted by a Sade disciple, often at full moon, intent on performing rituals close to the Marquis's heart.

'I like to look like a beggar when I work. This woman asked me whether the owner was satisfied with my work. I told her, "The Marquis trusts me completely."'

The shadow of the Marquis's ruined chateau

The woman confessed that she had often scaled the castle walls, penetrated the inner sanctum, and lain on her stomach on the cold stones.

'There she paid homage to the Marquis three times. Three times! She was a healthy young woman!'

Indeed, at sunset, or full moon, there is to me no more sacred a moment than to sit on the stone steps leading to the barred front door of the chateau, and consume, with tender delicacy, a modest sacrificial repast in honour of the Marquis. I feel he would approve of foie gras, little stuffed quails, and perhaps a sliver of peacock tongue.

Sade was, unsurprisingly, a supreme fantasist also in respect of food. There is no more intimate, and extreme, correlation between the delirium of food and of sex than in his fervid imaginings. Sexual pleasure combines orgasmically with tongue, taste, scent and gastric juices. In the most rapturous of his feasts, which are never distinguished from orgy, the food is spiced with succulent human bits, each prepared with great finesse. It is served by delectable naked virgins, each of them condemned to become a next course in turn. It is consumed on their very flesh, since the tables and chairs are made up of their suitably contorted bodies. Thus a stab to the buttock, a twirl to the breast, a tickle to the ribs, each mouthful eliciting savoury sighs and palpitations. What goes on between courses is too horrible to imagine, for those not made of stern stuff. But what a chef Sade would have made!

Christmas in Turkey

No turkey for Christmas, Christmas in Turkey! That was my happy cry as we churned through the Black Sea, tormented by yet another Mehmet or Ahmed with a cousin in the carpet business. This one plied us with tea until we felt like drowning, singing as he did so,

A sudden lobster fantasy: Linda at the Black Sea fishmarket

'*Chernobyl chai! Chernobyl chai!*' Don't ever let anyone tell you the Turk has no sense of humour.

When we disembarked, the sun was blazing like midsummer. The night before, in Cappadocia, it had snowed heavily, and we had been woken by the thump of a snowball on the window of our cave house, tossed by Ahmed (yes, I'm afraid so). He held in his hand a steaming bowl of fresh yogurt topped with wild honey, dotingly prepared by his wife for our breakfast. In all our time in Turkey, we hardly saw a woman (and when Linda came to the *hamam* with me, the loincloth strapped to the giant Turkish masseur almost fell to the floor), yet I can commend their yogurt highly.

The cuisine in general was rather staid and dull, at least in our budget cafés in remote places in the dead of winter. Our fellow diners looked emaciated with bulging eyes and stubbly faces, and used their fingers. The bread was horrible. But on the Black Sea, on Christmas Day, the fish market shimmered with colour and freshness. I had a sudden lobster fantasy, and approached the jolly lobster man in the international language of shrugs, furrowed brow, and gesticulating hands. He gave me a sum that my calculator translated as a hundred pounds. I gave a patronising smile. He repeated it. I corrected him by dividing his price by ten. Ten pounds for the lobster seemed astronomical to me, still in the thrall of Mrs Fish's five rand crayfish. The fisherman stuck to his dinars, and I sacrificed my lobster.

What we did find was a true fisherman's café, elevated and looking out to a sunlit sea, where we downed an embarrassing number of langoustines, as sweet and crisp as the midwinter light. They quite transformed our culinary view of Turkey. We were benignly immune to the chattering of another carpet salesman as the boat chugged back past the faded palaces of the Bosphorus in the twilight.

Langoustines, as sweet and crisp as the midwinter light

Banquet of Pigs

Segovia, in the south of Spain, is a city warm, organic, female, as open as a shell. The river meanders, crowned by the glorious Roman aqueduct, the castle turrets are gently rounded, the trees lacy and soft, there is perfume on the breeze. The atmosphere is Moorish, glowing sandstone, ornate stone fretwork. Even the winter light is warm.

There are many enticing reasons to come here. Above all, perhaps, to savour the rival gastronomy of the two famous restaurants that vie for supremacy, *Casa Duque* and *Candido*, the culinary Montague and Capulet of Castile. Their speciality is the suckling pig, and it is the finest in the world.

We tried the *Duque* first, a grand historical establishment which remains obliging and sedate. I must admit that we were not in the least put off by the rotund piglets curled deliciously on each platter. They looked sublimely content, positively sparkling with crisp succulence. The taste is the finest and softest you could imagine, like nibbling the juicy bits of a delicious baby.

Next night, we crossed to *Candido*, cobbled mosaic floors in a medieval building below the aqueduct. The haughty maitre d' looked askance when we said we had not booked, but ushered us to a table that could not have offered better entertainment. For there before us was a true banquet of pigs, a scene straight from *Animal Farm*, tearing and gobbling and grunting over their meal. Presiding over the table was none other than Candido himself, a porker of considerable substance. Not a word was uttered, all heads burrowing into the suckling pigs on their plates. Dog may well eat dog, but what we witnessed was pig eating pig. Candido's neck bulged with pink lard, his piggy eyes were deeply recessed, his jowls quivered with greed, as if this were the last pig of his life. It was evidently not the first. He had become what he ate, and, as Orwell observed, looking from man to pig it was impossible to tell one from the other.

It almost put us off our food, although perhaps it was unwise to tackle two such meals in a row.

The maitre d' remained huffy, minions hovered about Candido's grunting table, everyone else felt left out. On leaving, I asked a waiter if Candido ate like that every night. He looked nervous, and nodded. Candido shot a bleary, angry look in our direction.

'Tell Senor Candido,' I said to the waiter, 'that in the banquet of pigs, your patron is the best. But, when it comes to food, *Casa Duque* wins.'

The waiter quivered, probably did not understand, but I felt restored.

Pork with Fennel and Ginger

Never underestimate the good porker. It provides excellent meat, is apparently consoling for cholesterol twinges, and is versatile and succulent.

Roll a good belly of pork and stuff with exuberant sprouts of fennel. Salt and pepper generously. Score the rind deeply so you get a crisp crackling, and drizzle olive oil. Grate fresh ginger over the carcass, and wickedly insert some pieces into the openings. Roast on a bed of fennel. The aroma and taste are cause for rapture.

The Dwarf with Deep Pockets

The best restaurant in Florence is in an unprepossessing backstreet near the station. You will find it on account of the queue of people in the street, long before it opens. Those near the front are staring, not without resentment, at an unusual sight. The family, and their retainers, are seated at a banquet table gorging themselves on dinner. Not one of them bothers to lift his eyes to the throng

The dwarf with deep pockets

patiently waiting outside, some pressing their faces to the windows. The doors do not open until they are replete. Do not be discouraged. It is well worth the wait, and the insult.

The place fills instantly. Long tables, squashed together with strangers, open wine on the table, no menu. A buzz and hum of pure authenticity. Father slicing hams, dangling from hooks, with consummate artistry, fish in tanks, flagons of oil, scents and flavours heavy in the air.

We found ourselves next to rich bankers from London. They were on honeymoon, and bored us with the luxury hotels they had stayed in, the expensive food consumed. Here, they evidently thought they were slumming it for the sake of authenticity. But the food was wonderful. Course after course arrived, perhaps we ordered, perhaps it simply materialised. Even our world weary jet-setters had never tasted flavours so robust, subtle, and penetrating.

The whole riveting performance was overseen by one of the sons, Giovanni, a dwarf with huge, flapping (although short) trousers, who danced merrily on the tables. His party trick was to stuff great wads of notes, as customers paid up, into the trouser pockets. The trick was that the pockets went right down to his ankles, and would rapidly fill up as the evening progressed, until notes overflowed and fell down his legs. Giovanni, with a little flourish, would then begin on the other pocket, until he looked as if he had elephantiasis of the legs. When both legs were full, he waddled away and the evening was over.

When Giovanni came to settle with us, I had the familiar feeling of anxiety occasioned by Italian restaurants with delicious food but no menu. Giovanni accepted only cash for his almost bottomless pockets, so credit cards could not save us. With deft speed he squiggled a long list of hieroglyphics, a sharp appraising eye on the banker, and handed it to our fellow diners. The banker propped his specs on the end of his nose.

Then, to my utter consternation, blanched, and turned to his wife whispering hoarsely. They both began fumbling through their pockets. They were sweating. He raised an eyebrow at me, smiled bravely. The number of lira they finally produced looked enough to revive the Banco Ambrosia from ruin. Giovanni could hardly fit them into his pockets.

I was pulverised with fear. We had consumed plate for plate exactly what they had. Giovanni was scribbling madly, eyeing us now. He tossed me the bill. My eye swayed to the bottom line. My face crumpled. One of his tricks? It was ridiculously little. Was the banker a fraud?

I paid with alacrity. The banker did not notice what I paid, he still appeared stricken.

'Bloody hell,' he finally managed.

'What's that?' I suddenly felt superior.

'Pretty good. But pretty damn stiff. Makes the Gritti seem cheap.'

He pushed his bill across to me. It was four times ours, for the exact same meal. Giovanni's sharp little eyes had summed us up perfectly.

I couldn't resist my parting shot.

'Oh really? Do you think so? Seems reasonable enough to me.'

Linda and I swanned out into the night, feeling like Rothschilds.

L'Éclipse

I was right in line for the solar eclipse. Paco Rabanne, the Parisian couturier and panacea of French neurosis, made a complete arse of himself by predicting the end of the world, and fleeing to an undisclosed sanctuary. In grey, rain-sodden England, the lemmings made for Cornwall, where, predictably, the clouds closed in. In Reims, the sky was clear as champagne, and Jessie

Norman sashayed in to sing the praises of the eclipse in the Cathedral.

I was perfectly placed. Our friends had a champagne estate in a village outside Reims, the heart of Champagne, far enough from Paris to shake off the crowds, and directly in the path of the eclipse. Their stylish young friends, when asked what they did, rolled their eyes mysteriously and replied, '*Commerce* . . .' And when pressed further, '*Monsieur Versace* . . .', shrugging with false modesty. Each had brought different designer glasses to shield them from the eclipse. Everyone was so pleasantly tiddly on the home-grown champagne that it hardly mattered if there were an eclipse or not. It may well have been inside our heads.

As the shadow loomed, we donned glasses and craned our necks. As the sun shrank, there was a sense of curious reversal in which the sun became a waning moon, rapidly gobbled up by a voracious predator. At the climax, the last bite was taken and the sliver in the sky disappeared. In the middle of a summer's day, darkness, and a sudden chill. The Parisian boys reached for their designer jackets. There was an ominous sense as if a violent storm were about to break. Perhaps Paco was right.

There was a palpable eerie silence. Birds stopped singing, bees that had moments before been buzzing among the flowers fell silent. Dogs howled. The street lights came on. Imagine the world without the sun. Then a cock crowed, a sudden flight of birds across the sky. A chilly new dawn as the sun was unveiled, glowing through our glasses like a waxing moon. Night had lasted two minutes.

Richard, our young host, raised a glass.

'*Bon éclipse!*'

Dinner, around long scrubbed tables in the cellar, is a noisy French affair, with Maman dominating from the head of the table. Papa giggling with the champagne he knocks back, flapping his hands. There are many benign altercations, often over finer points in the production of their champagne, in which each side finally backs off with equal senses of justification.

'I like the champagne,' says Richard with a sense of melancholy. 'But I think I drink too much.'

Papa has prepared a barbecue, for which he has constructed an elaborate revolving grid attached to an ugly metal post like a gibbet. He piles on the vine stock and applies a blowtorch.

There is *merguez* and a variety of local sausages; burnt lamb chops and heaps of couscous and *taboule*. Baguettes naturally, and a number of whole brie cheeses. Several different fruit tarts made by Richard. Gazpacho to start. Papa pops champagne without a break, embracing everyone in turn, 'Ça va? Ça va?'

A loving cup circulates. It is a bottle sealed in foil.

'Drink, and look into the eyes of the person opposite you.'

We all do. A strong blast of alcohol, plum perhaps.

With a flourish, Richard unwraps the foil. In the bottle, doubled over and more or less filling it, is a striped dead snake.

'Viper,' laughs Richard, and swigs back the dregs in the bottle, sticking his tongue into the opening to touch the head of the snake. He cannot resist explaining that any blockage we might have felt as we took our draughts would have been the snake head against our tongues. One woman covers her head in her hands and screams, '*Non Richard! Arrêt!*'

My last view, as I lurch from the table, is Richard maniacally refilling the bottle with alcohol, ready for the next time.

Feast from Paris

The only consolation in leaving Paris is to hoard as many delicacies on the last morning as one's hand luggage can hold. I spend the last hours frenetically hurtling from the *boucherie* in rue Faubourg St Denis to the *fromagerie* at the top of rue Martyrs, and am readily distracted by every food emporium in between. I clutch at aged armagnacs, raspberry vinegar, and jars of *confiture de rose*. I cannot resist a tarte tatin from the *patisserie* in rue Montorgueil. Some special breads from *Chez Paul* next door.

I gather fresh foie gras and smoked duck breasts in slivers; plump *magrets de canard,* decadent *confits*, and pots of pâté de foie gras. They are reverently packaged for the long haul by butchers in white coats who look like professors of surgery. At the famous cheese shop, I am advised by the *maître* what is of a perfect ripeness to survive the flight and satisfy on arrival. All my hopes and fantasies are settled on the dinner I will give on the first night home. I take a whole Brillat-Savarin, the supreme Burgundian triple cream cheese, so rich that a single spoonful can knock out the faint-hearted. There is Pérail, the crust palpitating with viscosity, there is burnished Langres like molten lava, subtle Tamié, and Tomme de St Hilaine, fresh from the mountains. I take a tub of the creamiest crème fraiche imaginable. Each is packaged with the delicacy of rare antiquities, for that is what they are. I hold the cultural heritage of the country in my hands.

On the flight, my hoard is stashed in the overhead locker. A pungent, exhilarating aroma permeates the cabin as the hours drag by. Other passengers feel faint. At last we land.

The feast is held at Mae and Theuns's farm. Select friends beam in from far and wide. They pick up the aromas from miles away. Niels and Carey are there, Ali,

Johan, Bruce and Kate. We dig into the exquisite foie gras. It makes anything else seem pointlessly banal. Someone annoys me by smearing it thickly on the bread and exclaiming, *Nice pâté!*, as though he is eating liver spread. He will not be invited again.

The salad with smoked duck, to which I add dollops of the delicate rose petal jam, is a delight. The whole foie gras is sizzled for a moment with a dash of armagnac. Later, the cheeses, and chunks of *Paul's* breads, are a revelation. We groan as the tarte tatin slips down with lashings of crème fraiche. Nobody believes they will survive the night. We crawl to bed, quite content to die in our sleep, consoled by dreams of paradise.

I am already planning my next trip, and my return with my bag of delicacies.

Tarte Tatin

I am not a pudding man. Most men are, if surreptitiously, and women are unashamedly so. I ignore puddings on a menu, preferring an hors d'oeuvre, or the cheese board – better, as the French have it, *chariot* of cheese – any day.

This confession does not mean there are no exceptions. Happily, inconsistency prevails, and there are some fruit puddings which I do not resist. Supreme is the tarte tatin, a pudding that secures the French the culinary prize, simply in virtue of what they can do to an apple. There is a thrilling zest to the name: it trills off the tongue like a trumpet flourish: *ta-ta-ta-ta!* I often wander the streets of Paris in search of the perfect tarte tatin, and have been known to choose a restaurant on that strength alone. Which goes to show that I am perhaps a closet pudding man after all. I am unabashedly a tarte tatin man.

In the pan lay slivers of butter to cover, over which sprinkle six heaped tablespoons of castor sugar. Core the apples and slice them in half, sufficient to squeeze into the pan when you jam them in upright in concentric circles.

Turn up the heat so that the ingredients bubble fiercely and caramelise. A curious, one might almost say sexual, rhythm is achieved as the apples appear to ride the fluid. There is a sudden rush of caramel on the senses as the sauce comes to an amber syrup. Fondle the apples to check softness and remove to cool slightly.

Cover the pan with a chilled short crust pastry, which you have cut into a round slightly bigger than the pan. Tuck it in well on the inside – this is important – of the pan. Bung it in the oven at moderate heat for about twenty minutes until the pastry is done and turns the colour of cognac.

Now the moment of revelation which makes this apple dish so special. Turn the pan over and gently flip the pudding out on its back, so to speak. The lovely glowing apples smile up radiantly from their pastry base. Devour the entire tart with lashings of crème fraiche, and run your fingers about the pan for every last morsel. You will never have a finer pudding.

There are many variations of this great traditional dish, but this is the one that works best. I owe it to Barbara, who has devoted time and care to experimentation. As with all of her puddings, it is perfect. So much for my pretence at pudding aversion.

The Judgement of Noria

Noria Mabasa is the finest sculptor working in wood and clay in Venda. She is not only a woman (and the only one in an art dominated by men), but a woman of mystical, and psychic, powers. Noria dreams her creations, and then sets to work. She is famous, and her works dominate galleries, public spaces, and the Union Buildings, seat of government in Pretoria. Beneath all this, there is a woman of dignity, simplicity, and humour, whom it is a privilege to know.

One of Noria's most striking and original creations is

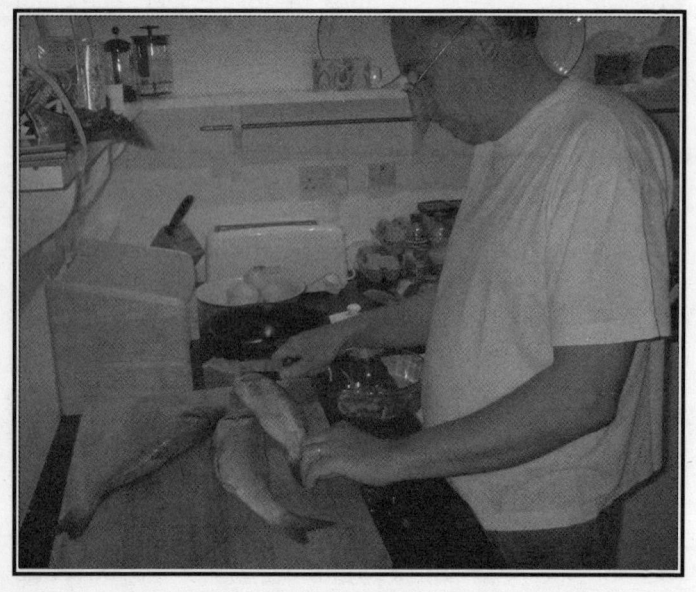

Bruce preparing Sea Bass in Cornwall

an entire Venda village at Lesheba in the Soutpansberg mountains. It is an art village, where Noria has transformed the skeleton of a traditional village into a fantasy of clay. It is one of the most remarkable sights in the country. Fatted oxen, lion and giraffe surround the space; human shapes and forms are sculpted into the contours of the huts and walls; a maiden gazes over the valley with the shower spout coming out of her ear. The chief sits serenely overseeing all, his gaze seeming to follow one's every move.

We brought Noria from her own village to spend a couple of days with us at the village she had created at Lesheba. She was delighted with its magic, as if she were seeing it freshly for the first time. Bruce and I cooked supper in the boma among flickering candles and a thousand moths. Bruce was doing his chicken with lemons, and the conversation and banter flowed like wine.

Noria was peculiarly animated, and riveted us with tales of superstition and folklore. She is an inspired storyteller, and Bruce was enthusiastically filming away in the candlelight as chubby crackled away in the oven. These are perhaps excuses why the supper took such ages to materialise. Finally, it was late and Noria began to weary. Quietly she slid aside and, almost unnoticed, prepared her own supper, deftly and without fuss. There was chicken, wild spinach, and perhaps a magic potion or two. She finished eating, looking well satisfied, long before we had even started.

At last, as she was preparing for bed, we insisted Noria taste our supper. It had been laborious, but we knew it would be good (Bruce never fails), and we were keen for Noria's accolade. She put her finger into the sauce. We eyed her keenly. She picked out a piece of chicken, tasted it. We looked anxiously for approval. Noria yawned.

'Mine was much better.'

She smiled and turned to bed. The artist had spoken, and we never felt quite the same again.

Lemon Bottom Chubby

Bruce says, take a few lemons and stuff 'em up the bum. He is speaking of the first, and almost last, step in the preparation of his naughty lemon chicken.

The lemons are halved prior to insertion, and salt and pepper are rubbed inside the carcass. More lemons are halved and quartered, and balanced in the creases and folds of chubby, which has been doused in olive oil. Some juice is squeezed over it, and chubby is roasted until golden, or lemon crisp. The gravy is made by adding a nugget of butter and some white wine to the juices. If you're in the mood, heat some brandy or Calvados and toss it flaming over the bird. The tang of lemon is not overwhelming, indeed is as clear and bracing as a night under the stars at Noria Mabasa's inspired village.

Millennium among the Lions

The big issue for me, as the century turned, was where to get away from the madding revellers. I was sick to death of all the hype and mystic bullshit, and prospects of crazed capitals spewing jamborees and fireworks (or, as some predicted, crashing to the ground) left me frightened and angry. I had to escape.

Fortunately, I found peace in the most ideal of all sanctuaries for the weary of spirit, the African bush. There is nothing that has the same power to revive, transform and heal, and it is the one element that I truly pine for as I roam other parts of the world. It has something to do with putting things in perspective, humility and balance, and it is profoundly regenerating.

Marco is an emblem of the natural man, and I envy him his life among the lions and maroela trees. In Timbavati, he lives in touch with basic instincts and connections. He told us that there is a Small Five too: the ant lion, buffalo weaver, leopard tortoise, elephant shrew, and rhino beetle. We sat around the fire in the boma, in the mellow trance of contentedness that the bush imparts, screened by tall reeds that do not keep out the mysterious sounds and scents of the bush. The earth rumbles from distant lions, mad hyena cries, coughs of antelope. A myriad more subtle tremors and invisible presences in the darkness.

We ate from a *potjie* brimming with hunks of *rooibok*, warthog, and giraffe. I felt sorry for the giraffe, and hoped he had died a natural death. His flesh, as it was, did not impress. The buck and hog were delicious. The meal was enhanced beyond any mere description of its ingredients and tastes, its slow brewing in a cast iron pot over the open fire, by the wild, electrifying magic of its setting. The night, alive with stars such as one never imagines in the city, susurrations and vibrations, the breeze that brings goosebumps, the glorious void of human traffic, filth and chatter, this is what made our Millennium a real transformation, a watershed in life, a return to true roots. We had no idea when midnight fell.

3

PRINCIPLES

To take pleasure in food, as I do, and to indulge the complex matrix of sensations that surrounds it, puts food in a broader context than mere cooking and eating.

I believe that interest in food is part of a bigger picture, the framework of one's tastes and proclivities, values and passions. The picture, essentially, of oneself.

I am taking the liberty of putting forward some ideas which ground my own passion for food in a broader context, exploring ways in which food relates to the pattern of one's life. Many of these strands have already emerged. I connect food to sex and to sensuality, and I have some thoughts on the notions of romance and art in respect of food. I am not trying to be comprehensive or too serious, nor struggling for spurious depth, but offer for your delectation some tantalising suggestions and whimsical fantasies, food for thought.

Sex and Food

We are sexual beings, more so than we sometimes admit. Sex is a big word, much bigger than what happens between the sheets or, as I might say, over the kitchen table. Sex is a matter of mind, outlook, instinct, demeanour, taste. It reveals itself in every gesture, decision, purpose and choice. It is what we look and listen for, what moves us and what we feel. It is the scent in our nostrils and the taste on our tongues. It is the very air that we breathe.

That is why we look at the sunset, gaze into the mirror, light candles, eat together, discuss books and movies and art. It is why we look at paintings and listen to music. It is why we are romantic, sensual, and moody. It is why we have relationships and why they end. It is why we get up in the morning. It is often why we go to bed.

Sex is everywhere. It's no more sex than sun on the grass is sex, says D H Lawrence.

What we are looking at is sex in a wider sense than the narrow one that impels the sexual act. That, too, is part of the sexual matrix, but it is only a part. There is much more to sex, and our sexual lives, than that. Sex begins in the brain, and it controls our lives. I don't mean to say that we are *literally* driven by sex in all the things that we do, although we should be in some of them, probably the most important ones. My understanding is rather that our sexuality *writ large* underlies and governs just about everything, whether we know it or not. It is the source of our compatibilities, and of our differences. It is the source of taste.

When it comes to food, we have sex translated into a context that is basic to our sustenance and survival. The desire to eat is more basic, more compelling, and most times more gratifying in execution, than the desire for sex. We certainly devote more time to it, and sometimes greater concentration and effort.

Sex may well be a passing phase; nobody would deny that its pleasure palls. Perhaps our sexual needs require constant renewal and change, perhaps there is simply not enough in the act to inspire prolonged interest, perhaps the structure of relationships is at fault, perhaps we lack imagination or simply do not know ourselves sufficiently in a sexual sense; whatever the caveats, food is a desire rooted in reality, where sex thrives on fantasy. We are wedded to food where marriages fail. Without food we perish; without sex we merely dry up. Stomach rules over groin, and food, of course, is the conduit to the heart.

Food is Sexy

Food is the sexiest thing in the world. We put our passion and our taste into it, we do it for the love of it, and for lovers. We make it beautiful, and we want to share it. Making food is a kind of lovemaking. It is the beginning of a lifelong romance, not least with oneself.

Just as sex defines our taste, so does food. Tell me what you eat, and I'll tell you what you are. One look at your shopping trolley will give you away. I'll certainly know if I want to have sex with you.

We are choosy and partisan, huffy and committed, enthusiastic and stand-offish, pernickety, passionate, and cold as frozen fish. Each of our moods, attributes, emotions, are expressed towards food as they are towards lovers. In each, we know, more clearly than in any other area of life, what we like, and what we cannot stomach. It is not a matter of words, much is unspoken, perhaps unsayable. Food, like sex, expands the spirit, and makes life, while it lasts, vibrate and glow.

We can be turned on, and off, by apparently negligible traces, variations and nuances, the merest suggestion or whiff, and it is all highly personal, even neurotic. That smile, the way the eyebrow shifts, the dimple, the way she mounts the stairs. I like brunettes; you, blondes. I'm a bottom man; you, breasts. Look at his hands. The eyes count first. With food, we are equally faddish, fetishistic, ourselves. Our tastes are an expression of ourselves, that is why we have to be so particular. In

Food is the sexiest thing in the world

making distinctions and choices, we are protecting ourselves, avoiding indigestion. There is all the difference in the world between the T-bone steak (with eggs and chips) and the duck *mousseline*, and it is not only to be found in the food.

People live or die by food, and by their particular choices and tastes. Lovers should be chosen by what they eat. Relationships are made, and fall apart. No finer way to connect than through a shared passion for food, and the same kind of food. No readier way to disagree. We can sometimes survive conflicts in other areas of mutual concern, we can argue, and agree to disagree. Even with art, where deep disagreements often tear relationships to shreds, we can sometimes survive, although with a revised perspective on our partner. It is always dangerous to share your favourite book or movie with a new lover. And you should tread especially warily when it comes to food. It is wise to share a meal before committing yourself to the same bed.

These are the two essential questions to ask of any lover, and the earlier you ask them the better for your appetites. What is food? What is sex?

The answers will sound much the same, at least will touch on the same deep vein of life. They will reveal what you need to know of your lover, the vital core, the deep taste, the inner life. Indeed, they point to, and frame, the biggest question of them all. What is living?

Appetite

We eat, we make love. These are primal appetites, and we enjoy an appetite for life. We crave, indulge, and are satiated.

Appetite is not hunger. Hunger is the primitive state. It has no allure, no glamour, no sophistication. It is uncontrollable, gnawing, and potentially fatal. You cannot doubt hunger, and it does not go away. We starve if it is not satisfied. People are starved of love too, and hungry for sex. It is not an appetising prospect.

Hunger is merely there, natural and rumbling; appetite needs to be aroused. Children have the primitive state, they are always hungry, and there is some lack of discrimination in what they wolf down.

As we grow up (no more growing pains, or hunger pangs), we become more discerning. We pick and choose, develop tastes and aversions. Appetite is more sporadic, and we play games with it. It comes and goes, and is influenced by context. We more often respond to some form of titillation to pique the palate. This might be an aroma, a visual image, or a verbal depiction. *Mmm, that smells, looks, sounds good!* Sometimes it is an association with a particular context or person. A favourite place can stimulate appetite, as can a person, particularly if that person is a lover, or potential lover.

So appetite is aroused. We come to food, as we do to love, with a sense of anticipation; the greater it is, the more we are aroused. We come to food as lovers. We hardly ever come upon it unprepared or by chance, as if stumbled upon, unless we are starving. Even a blind date has forewarning.

Our taste buds are as primed as sexual organs: we salivate, drool, lick our lips, our very tongues hang out ... The desires for food and for sex are each stimulated by an appetite to absorb and ingest, derive nourishment and satisfaction.

The best relationships are founded on a mutual appetite, and the more compatible the tastes the better. My one long affair with a vegetarian floundered every time I stabbed a loin of veal, each time she burped over the lentils. Choose your lovers like meals.

We salivate, drool, lick our lips ...

Foreplay

The body craves sensual stimulation, and it gets it from food and from sex. In each case, the approach is essential to the outcome. The *wham bam* approach makes for indigestion with food, indifference and premature ejaculation when it comes to sex.

Delicacy is the key: a slow, lingering, mounting sense of excitement towards crescendo. There are sex manuals galore, so I hardly need spell out tips for the sexually desperate, save for the obvious homily that it is always sensitivity towards the other that achieves satisfaction for both, and that slow is better than fast.

We move through the stages of a meal in a vocabulary that sounds sexual. Arousal, stimulation, absorption, sighs of contentment and gratification. *Ah! Mmm! Oh yes!* There is climax, and food should taste orgasmic.

It begins with a sense of foreplay and arousal, in the marketplace, always preferable to the supermarket. There is nothing as arousing as looking for food in a French market, for example, where food is elevated to a spectacle that is overpoweringly seductive. It gives a new perspective to the dreary word *shopping*, extending an imaginative dimension that is irresistibly tempting. It is a wholly sensuous experience.

The radiance of fruit and vegetables cannot be imagined by those unfortunate enough to drag themselves through the tiresome predictability and sterility of supermarkets. Apricots glowing like the dawn, peaches like perfect posteriors, the crisp tang of apples, rotund oranges and curvaceous pears, raspberries like garnets, wild strawberries from the forest, blackberries and blueberries darkly glowering. Every bright colour radiating from each stall under a striped canopy, the holder calling out his prices, darting to and fro like a dancer. Robust clutches of celery, leeks, carrots, radishes and asparagus; heaped piles of potatoes, courgettes,

Delicacy is the key

cauliflowers and marrows. Fragrant bunches of herbs, scenting the air. Pumpkins, melons and lemons shimmering in the sunshine.

One ricochets from stall to stall in a sensuous trance of delight. Cheeses, pâtés, tapenades, olives and olive oils; hams and sausages, chickens and pheasants and ducks, the finery of feathers and flesh. Breads of many shapes, textures and ingredients, no meal complete without one. Fish glistening and bright-eyed, *coquilles*, oysters, mussels and prawns on ice. *Pâtisseries* that display the artistry and finesse of generations of meticulous craftmanship. The wicker basket groans. It is never big enough.

One staggers home. It is like unpacking a trove of treasure. The French have no scruples about handling food, feeling the textures and ripeness in the fingers. The butcher will run the steaks and sausages through his fingers, and they will be pummelled and sniffed by the purchasers in turn. Tossed aside with a wry contortion of the face if not found to be exactly right. Fruits are arranged like flowers and may not be touched. They have already been tested for perfection by the vendor. But when you get home you fondle them as if they were flesh.

Quite overcome by the raptures of the market, it is refreshing to take a breather, ideally with a glass of cool wine under a beech tree in the garden, before tackling the second stage of foreplay, the rituals of preparation. This *is* beginning to sound like a sex manual – as we move delicately from base one to base two ...

Getting a meal together with your food paramour is a high point in the day's traffickings, best at night when making dinner together approximates a sexual act, and is often a prelude to one. Each slice to the tight skin of the tomato, each slap to the schnitzel and squeeze to the fillet, each finger dipped into the sauce, the scent of mushroom, each dollop of crème fraiche to the lips ...

You need good pots and pans, and a concentrated battery of quality implements. I have listed most of them at the end of this chapter. It is important to derive pleasure from the utensils, so spare time to select the most appropriate. There is nothing to match the glow of copper. I take great pleasure in getting a meal together, especially if it is for close friends and loved ones. There is a sense of doing it to gratify them, and it opens a channel of contact and interplay that has its own intimacy and satisfaction. All the better if the preparations are shared, where one finds that working together on the food draws one the closer in other respects. The conversation flows, the wine slips down, hands touch, there is a mood of sensual accord, and the meal is concocted.

If there is no lover to share the experience, then corral your guests in the kitchen, quaffing wine with admiring exchanges on your feats of culinary conjuring. This is good for the ego and showing off, and makes guests believe they are contributing to the occasion. There is a pleasantly conspiratorial mounting of expectancy. Brush aside offers to help, they will ruin your efforts. Indeed they are never meant to be taken seriously. When it comes to washing up never believe protestations of assistance; they might be well intentioned but their refusal is always met with relief.

The design of the meal should reflect a movement from subtle arousal to climax. That is why there are starters, and that they are as they are. Light, tantalising, piquing the appetite for the more substantial thrust of the main course. Thought is given to the ways in which flavours and courses combine. In food, as in love, rhythm and compatibility are essential. Check with your partner. Clashing tastes, combinations that jar, strident differences in texture and bulk ... plan the transition from start to finish with subtlety and finesse. You don't want to come to it too quickly, or from the wrong angle, or with mistaken assumptions. No good to start with fish and move on to fish. The taste of grapefruit does not go well with asparagus. Tomato in the gazpacho, not also in the stew. Cream sauce with the duck is too rich. A light pudding to finish off. There are vegan lovers too.

The setting is vital to the final effect, and is an essential ingredient in the foreplay to the meal. It can make or break it, however much consideration has gone into the food. A sensual touch is required. Pay attention to the cutlery, as you did to the cooking utensils. Food always tastes better with good cutlery. If you have silver, use it. That is what it is there for, to enhance the experience; it is pointless to stash it in the bank vault. Throw out the nasty aluminium; never use plastic (it would be better to eat with your fingers). Get an attractive set of crockery, it will also make the food taste and look better. Serving dishes are infinitely better than cooking pots on the table (unless they are copper, or if the food is appropriate to the dish, such as paella – where the food actually takes its name from the dish). Linen and napkins enhance the effect too. Get the lighting right, it is a question of mood. Nobody likes eating under harsh light, not even sunlight; neon is completely indigestible. Light the candles.

The whole idea is to *make something special* with food, elevate it from the ordinary and mundane, and it does not require much effort. Attitude and a sense of style make the difference. Food is otherwise a routine and a bore. It is well to remember with food, as with sex, the undeniable truth: live for the day, for tomorrow we die! Make the most of the meal. You never know, it may be your last.

Foreplay relies on temptation, and there is nothing easier to give in to. Get the mood right, pay attention to nuance and detail, plan with subtlety, put in effort and care, and he or she is yours for the eating. The injunction for food is the same as for sex: don't gobble. Take it slow, pace yourself, savour each lingering moment. Nibble, suck, lick, and smack the lips. Draw it out, it's all there is, and it doesn't last long. Not nearly long enough.

Climax

Not all climaxes are equal. Nor are they the same. They derive from foreplay, and rely on pacing. They vary from the almost imperceptible, the exquisitely subtle, to the big bang. Tastes vary, and variety is desirable. A need for a gossamer soufflé is right at one place and time, a rich and heady beef stew at another. It is not a matter of comparison or superiority, more one of occasion and nuance. One finds that one's sexual diet requires as much consideration, which includes range and variety, as one's meals. Favourites endure, there might be a perennial pattern, but what happens on the fringe, the unexpected, and the anticipation of what might still be to come, provide fresh succour.

What counts as climax? As with sex, it is subtle, and it might be instantaneous. It can be a touch, like the moment the lip touches the foie gras, or the tongue curls round the oyster. Perhaps it is delayed until the chocolate soufflé. A meal is orchestrated like a symphony. There are movements that vary in mood and tempo, and satisfactions are found at different points. The important issue is that the whole experience hangs together; the sense that one has been seduced by a master of the art.

It would be interesting (food for thought) to speculate on how one's tastes in food correlate and climax with one's tastes in love. Does the fact that I am a devotee of chicken in all its guises, but that I would cry out for crayfish on my deathbed, say anything about my rollercoaster love life? I do not set much store by desserts and do not have a sweet tooth. Starters have their place, but I am a main course man. There is variety in my main course repertoire, but I return to well-tested favourites, partly for the comfort of familiarity. One cannot adventure all the time. I could not stomach crayfish more than occasionally. Its exoticism is partly what makes it climactic.

My selections are not particularly exotic or complex, in fact I prize simplicity, and my electives are conservative. The aesthetic element is strong: I like the way food looks. I concentrate on the elements of foreplay. I am experimental within a rather rooted framework. I don't like wasting time and tend to be spontaneous and direct. I am easily bored by the same routine, so am tempted to add a dash of this or that here and there. I enjoy the untried and unusual sometimes at a restaurant. I do not like to eat at a restaurant anything I have at home, or believe I could produce better myself. Ah yes, the restaurant is my brothel ... Does this begin to sound like confession? We have not yet reached the end.

Afterglow

To every climax, there is an afterglow. To some, it is in the calm that follows the storm that true repose is found. Forget the hurly-burly, the cut and thrust, *sturm und drang*: the mature vision is the contemplative one, the relief afforded to the struggle. I begin to sound old.

Nevertheless, to many foodies, dessert is the true highlight, the afterglow, the sweet surrender that follows rapture. The French, cunning in food as in love, prolong the afterglow until after the cheese, itself a heavy course which might also be seen as the climax of the meal. Cheese, after all, is the true glory of French culture. Nevertheless, the exquisite effort and detail in French *pâtisseries* speaks for itself. The conservative English tradition, which comes immediately to the sweet repose and ends on the heavy note of cheese, might also be seen as a direct reflection of national character. And English puds are generally stodgy and sickly sweet.

Everyone finds his or her own mark. Women, it is said, are weaker (in the sense of craving more – which I suppose really means that they are stronger) when it comes to dessert. They have the sweeter tooth, the sugar and spice and all things nice. I have never found this to be true, in respect of dessert. Perhaps it is one of the burdens men have imposed in their perception of the sweeter sex. Most men I know go for dessert with as much gusto (and less delicacy) as their paramours. I suppose it is important, to you and to your lover, to determine whether you are essentially a dessert or a main course person. Perhaps it changes. All I know is that I have never met a starter person, nor would want to.

Good and Bad

The differences between good and bad in food and sex are closely allied. Good in each case takes care and shows respect for the ingredients, gives attention to detail and nuance, atmosphere and mood, and seeks a context that supports and enhances the act. Neither food nor sex is good in isolation, under distasteful circumstances, or with the wrong ingredients. The urge to create good food and to have good sex is driven by passion, enthusiasm, imagination and flair; and practice is essential. Great chefs make great lovers.

So dull cooks make dull lovers, and dull lovers are not worth cooking for. What is missing is the spark that transforms the ordinary into the singular. We all want to feel special, yet it is easy to rest on assumptions and habits, where the price exacted is boredom. It is in the urge to explore and create something new and stimulating that desire is awakened, and the significance of cooking and sex begin to make sense. We are what we eat as much as who we eat. Food is self-expression and a love affair with oneself. It is also the best way out of oneself, and into the other.

We remember bad experiences more clearly than we do good ones, unless they are very good indeed. Thus memorable meals stand out, and the sense lingers, as do significant lovers. We might not have exact recall, but what we do remember is enough to set our hearts and palates aglow way into the future. Often it is enough simply to recall that smile, that moment, that scent, that look, flavour or aroma, the singular thing that still strikes to the core long after the experience has faded. It is notoriously difficult to recall taste; vision, even scent, is conjured up far more readily. That is why lovers linger longer in the memory than meals, except that they are often recalled with pain, whereas a great meal leaves a trace only of happiness.

It is as dispiriting to see food as a dreary daily grind as it is to have a dull sexual routine – habits between clenched teeth. Each needs to be raised to the power of desire for the appetites to be fulfilled. The housewife who resentfully turns out microwave food for her stolid family finds herself in much the same situation between the sheets. Everyone suffers as food and sex take their weary toll, and this for most people is what food and sex – life itself! – is about.

The *merely* good, we hardly remember with clarity. Perhaps it is our expectation, so we do not pause to appreciate it, perhaps it happens too often, and so blurs into the hazy sense of well-being and low profile contentment that we take to be sufficient for life. But the thrilling, and original, detail is missing, the searing force. Bad categories, though, rankle, fester, and endure. We never return to a restaurant where we had a bad meal. We are tempted to eschew the dinners of friends who cook badly. We bear scars from bad experiences in love.

That is not to say that we do not learn from bad, as much as from good. It might well be said that we cannot profit from the good unless we have acquaintance with the bad, for otherwise how could we tell the difference? The good sets examples to emulate and cherish. The bad teaches us, sometimes, what to avoid, and other times, things about ourselves and what we pursue as our sense of good. We move, in both cases, from innocence to experience. Yet there is a salient difference between bad love and bad food. We learn from the latter, what to avoid and how not to do it. When it comes to bad experience in love, it does not appear to translate well, nor set warning bells ringing, in our subsequent experience. We do not see it coming next time round, and step into that same murky old river time and again. Perhaps in love all bad experiences are different, whereas in food they are the same. We do not learn from love as we do from food.

On the Young

The beginnings in babyhood are not auspicious. All that puréed pumpkin. Mush will come of mush, and whereas there might be reason for it early on, the progress from nappyhood should be matched with dramatic change of diet. The habits of babyhood need to be unlearned.

What usually happens is that the diet of mush is replaced by one of stodge. Children imitate their elders. If you eat crap, so will your kids. They may well eat crap anyway, and be unaware of it. The palate needs to be educated, just like any other taste. Resistance should be overcome.

The best method is not necessarily force-feeding, although with some kids I am sorely tempted. James will eat nothing green, Ollie nothing wild, Margo will not touch an egg, unless it's a perfect omelette, in which case she doesn't believe it's an egg at all. Talk, explain,

Mae, Margo and Simone

encourage, experiment. There is nothing that should be rejected out of hand, everything should be tried. It is often necessary to try more than once; persistence can pay off.

I remember dear Mae as a salutary case. Mae who never ate oysters because she never had, and the thought repelled. That live writhe at the epiglottis. So she desisted over the year we shared in Paris. As often as I could, I crammed oysters down my throat, straight from the fishmonger's iced tables in the Rue Montorgueil, on the banks of the Seine, washed down with Chablis. All the while Mae looked on with indifference, perhaps repulsion, a choking sensation at the back of her throat, chewing at her baguette and cheese.

It was not until she was seduced by a liberated culinary lover, later to be husband, bearing oysters, that she saw the error of her ways and the regrettable waste of opportunity. As so often, sex and food merged in a moment of passion. She set to right the privations of the past with gusto, even taking over a lodge close to Knysna to scent the oysters in the breath of the lagoon. They were downed by the platterful and truckload, and the passion was passed on to her young daughters, who held the record for oyster consumption by babies in the western world. I have an enduring image of Mae and Theuns looking on with wide-eyed adoration and without trace of resentment, as Margo and Simone stuffed down the last handful of glistening oysters, the last few the poor parents had intended for themselves. It was a moment of intense, almost tragic, self-sacrifice.

I am not sure of the wisdom of this. My question to Mae was how her children would survive into adulthood unless their great oyster expectations were met. Did not an inevitable oysterless wilderness stretch ahead? Nurtured on oysters, how might they survive on less? Mae's answer was that they should know the best in order to expect the best, the earlier the better. Oysters should be suckled on the teat. I must say it seemed a simple pleasure, churlish to deny.

On the subject of children in restaurants, I fear I shall give some offence, probably also to my dearly besotted friends. Restaurants are not for children. The only exceptions should be treats, rare occasions, where the children are rehearsed, smartened up, and impeccably behaved. You can see the excitement glistening in their eyes. In that way, their presence is tolerable to adults in the place, and they meld seamlessly with the environment.

One recalls with horror the days and, worse, nights, when one was assailed – visually and aurally – by the hideousness of other people's mismanaged children. This is a simple truth – recognised by everyone who does not bask in the glory of parenthood, and often by those who do, at least in respect of children other than their own – that the only children one can bear unleashed in an adult context, or one in which one would rather be alone, are one's own.

Believe it or not, I actually think such a change of attitude – impossible to realise, I quite appreciate – which doting parents may well find intolerant, not to say intolerable, is to the benefit of the child. It is certainly a blessed relief to every other restaurant diner. For the child, though, it surely has the benefit of inculcating a sense of proportion and value. It encourages the belief that the world is not simply an open cheque book (daddy's), nor simply a materialistic waste of time. It may be said to be an antidote to the despair in adulthood that will inevitably follow such a course.

Treats should be distinguished from ordinary fare, and special occasions seen to be special. They will then be cherished, savoured, and the next time looked forward to. Boredom is the great enemy, and it follows as naturally from indulgence as does the unpleasant belch from the hamburger. My antidote is an education in discriminating good from bad, right from wrong, and the earlier it takes shape the better. This moral education should gel with an education of the senses and tastes, and perhaps it starts there. We certainly set out as feelers and suckers and sniffers, before becoming thinkers and worriers. The sense of discrimination is essential to leading any kind of life at all, and it needs discipline to grow. We could make no move or decision without it, and assume it in everything we do. The task is to make our closet set of such values more explicit, and bolder. The stronger and more worked out the set, the more likely the chance of leading a better, even wiser, life, with a finer sense of appreciation, and a real – as opposed to merely materialistic – sense of value.

There is all the difference in the world between value and price. Children indulged thoughtlessly, in restaurants and in every other respect, cannot learn that difference. The sense of value is quite literally spoiled. They know the price (they can read the menu), but have no sense of the value. Perhaps they cannot tell the difference between the prawn starter or the grapefruit, except that one costs more than the other. Price is a material matter, and it should have to be earned. Value is what is important, if one is to grow and flourish, in any but a material way. There is more to life than the price on the menu.

It might be difficult for parents to resist pressure from their children, and their own peers, and perhaps some feel they don't want to stint their kids, even that spoiling them is good. My parents couldn't afford it, but I can! One shows off one's material success through indulgence of one's children, who become emblems of one's power. Yet, when it comes to food, I see a difference between a tiny palate and a mature one, and I think there is a process in getting from one to the other which involves time and experience. There are analogous arguments in respect of sex, and I doubt that the joys of prepubescent sex would be blithely endorsed by the same parents who force-feed their offspring foie gras and lobsters. And, call me a retrograde old bastard, but the prospect of kids stuffing them down their throats sticks not so much in their gullets as my own. They have nothing in the world to look forward to.

The Peter Pan Principle

Food equates with life, living to the full, liveliness. It is the dream pursuit of eternal life which, for the most part, boils down to the quest for youthfulness, the desire to stay forever young, at least at heart and in the taste buds. It is there, above all, that one feels one is alive. Food, like sex, is part of the Peter Pan principle of life, and its pursuit is everything. Fantasy is often more compelling than reality.

It is a thrill to pass on the secrets of the kitchen to eager inheritors. The urge to inherit is not natural, it has to be inculcated. Temptation always works. As with language, music, and perhaps everything else, the channels are more open when young. Taste buds are unformed and can dry up without ever salivating. It is a process that has to be learned. It is therefore appropriate to inculcate a passion for food in the young. One's experience of food is indubitably enhanced by the presence of youth. They help to stave off the sense of an ending. For the end of food is of course the end of life.

There is consolation in relying on the young to cheer one up, in the face of creaking age, dulling palate and flagging sex. A hand-picked smattering of youth is vital to spice up one's (increasingly) geriatric dinner parties. The evening will inevitably be ruined by the old, who chomp away, turn the music down, fall asleep over dinner, and need to go home early. Turn to the young for stimulation, and indeed foreplay in the preparation of the food.

For help with menial tasks – and if you have the teaching urge – turn to the young, who after all have everything to learn. Not just any young of course, make them feel special, and select with care. There are always more rejects than acolytes. Concentrate on those who imbibe the aromas, tastes, touch and sight of food with a fresh and eager palate. Don't waste time with the inane and sulky-palated. Educate or banish. Give them pocket money to stuff themselves with msg and cholesterol junk. Young assistants in the kitchen run and fetch and watch and stir, salivating with excitement. Collar them while their eyes are still starry and there is a glow on the cheeks, before recalcitrance strikes them dumb, self-conscious, and *cool*. How many times must I remind them that food, like sex, is not cool. It's *hot*.

Oliver, my delightfully irreverent and original nephew, has a penchant for inverting names, thus he becomes Revilo, and I (with not so perfect reversal) Noj. He spills the flour and gets the yolk mixed with the shell, but his insouciant charm makes up for everything. He is eager to hurl the pasta to the wall to test its consistency, inevitably too soon. He throws himself across the table screaming, 'I'm useless, Noj! I should be shot!' My beautiful nieces, Margo and Simone, scrunch their fingers in the stuffing before plunging them into the duck's bottom with cries of delight.

Aphrodite Rises from the Waves

Truth is, all food has the seductive power of Aphrodite. It is our aspiration to rise to the power of the goddess, whose sensational birth yokes the idea of food to sexuality in the image of the aphrodisiac.

In the myth, Aphrodite rose from the sea and stepped serenely out of her shell (a mussel), her waist girded with the magic potions of love. She was created as the severed penis of Uranus, lord of the heavens, was hurled into the sea by his son Kronos, in vengeance for his father's slaying of all his other children. The sea foamed and spewed and churned as Uranus's mighty penis writhed in the waves. And out of the turbulence of foam stepped the goddess of love, bearing her girdle of sexual charms. There could hardly be a more Freudian moment.

Food, eating, ingestion is no doubt part of our sensual experience, but it should not be taken too literally. Fuss is sometimes made over the purportedly sensual, even highly sexual, qualities of some foods. It is all nonsense. The point to make is that the aphrodisiac sense is in the imagination, not in the food. It is what the imagination does to the food, endowing it with a sensual or sexual enticement. The senses are in tune, appetites are aroused, taste buds stimulated and the flow of juices is liberated. One is seduced into a good meal from the tip of the tongue to the tip of the toes. One comes to food as a lover.

Traditionally there are hackneyed contesters for aphrodisiacs, as if the sense were in the food itself. Oysters always come up, no doubt because they are swallowed alive, provoking ready sexual analogies; and we know how champagne is meant to loosen inhibitions. Asparagus, which must rely on the phallic association, although it is rather the strange scent imparted to the pee that lingers in the air. Artichokes, for obscure reasons (the heart, the bottom?), smoked salmon (vulva-pink perhaps; more likely, as with caviar, it is simply expensive), mussels (pornography on the table), even steak tartare (all that raw flesh). They are all absurd, except for the force of suggestion triggered in the mind.

More original contenders, flights of fantasy, come from literary sources, the most diverting of which is Norman Douglas's *Venus in the Kitchen*, where Pie of Bulls' Testicles (note, bulls' plural) settles gently with Sow's Vulva (marinaded in white wine). The anatomical correlation between food and sex could hardly be more wryly made. Such amusements are hardly intended to be taken literally. It changes things completely when they are.

The predations for taking aphrodisiacs seriously make one despair at human ghastliness, and the hideous distortions between food and sex that they concoct. The ruthless slaughter of Bengal tigers in order to grind their penises into potions, of Central African chimpanzees and gorillas scalped for their brains, of rhinos machine-gunned for their horns to console penile-challenged orientals, these are hideous debasements of the human spirit and its predatory psychoses.

We Eat What We Love

Loving what we eat is one thing, and sounds desirable. Change the desire around and it can stick in the throat. Eating what we love is strictly a matter for vegetarians.

Take the case of Yuko Hisho, who was the Japanese student in Paris who gained notoriety of a peculiar kind when he murdered his Dutch girlfriend, cut her into succulent joints with a fine butcher's art, and prepared every bit of her in different culinary ways, each dish according to the part, or perhaps each part according to the dish. Some of her had to be boiled for a long time; there were roasts, fricassées, stews and – this being a Japanese story – sushi, the delicate titbits particularly relished by Yuko Hisho, erotic chef extraordinaire, the lover who had turned his love to food. The unfortunate woman, his late lover, was stored in the freezer so that the feast could be prolonged, and it was there that the police found the clues to the odd smells that neighbours had reported. The Dutch shuddered with horror and deported Mr Hisho, the cannibal, to face the consequences at home in Japan.

What transpired shocked them as much as had the cannibalism. For Yuko Hisho stepped off the plane in Japan to a hero's welcome, was fêted by the media as a celebrity, and soon had his own television show, cookery of course. He went on to write cookery books (unashamedly, with titles like *Cannibalistic Fantasies*), and regale journalists with memories of the finest meal of his life. He said that the flesh of his victim melted in his mouth like raw tuna. I read a report of an interview with a female journalist who suddenly noticed a hungry glint in Mr Hisho's eye, and hurriedly crossed her legs. The last report indicated that he had made an erotic video called *The Desire to be Eaten*.

This extraordinary denouement is comprehensible only in cultural terms. It is in this sense that Mr Hisho might be seen as a victim of his inheritance, although hardly one that attracts sympathy. The case rests on the Japanese attitude to sexuality. Quite bluntly, the victim was a foreigner and she was a woman. Thus she was more or less dirt. Mr Hisho was wise enough to play out his fantasy with a Dutch girl in Paris.

Gruesome as the act was, it is perhaps not so hard to understand, if indeed rather hard to swallow. We all experience as lovers a frisson, rather than a shudder, of what impelled Mr Hisho's cannibalistic orgy. We kiss, lick, engorge, nibble and bite; we devour our lovers, in our imagination, like meals. There is the desire to make ourselves one flesh. Is it simply that we know when to stop, where to set the limits? Our own more modest senses struggle to accept Mr Hisho's more extraordinary ones.

In violating taboos of sexuality as much as food, and bringing them together in a particularly grisly brew, Hisho's tastes appear shocking, outrageous. Perhaps he simply did not distinguish sufficiently firmly the divide between imagination and reality. Perhaps he took fantasy too seriously, perhaps he was simply over-imaginative. He lacked proportion, and violated a strong taboo. His sense of taste, he might claim, got the better of him. But this is not simply a matter of taste, nor appetite. His act and our reaction are rooted in cultural and moral frameworks. The distance between culinary exploit and exploitative cuisine is worth preserving.

This is not a unique case. Many American serial killers have devoured their victims, often pleading love in mitigation. There is no surer way to keep the other for ever than to become one flesh. We digest our lovers like meals. Jeffrey Dahmer notoriously admitted to saving the heart of one of his victim lovers for last, the more intimately to prolong the affair. There could hardly be a clearer correlation between sex and food: getting to the heart of the matter without metaphor.

More recently, as a salacious titbit to the all-devouring web, we have cannibals disporting themselves on the Internet. For every predatory cannibal, there are hundreds of succulent morsels floating in the ether, eager to be devoured. Throw out the bait, and the wannabe morsels impale themselves with abandon. It has become an intriguingly voguish cyber-crime, making mincemeat, so to speak, of dreary old P D James and Inspector Morse, who now read like Enid Blyton. Bizarre murder always reads more like fiction than fact, but it can make a legend of the perpetrator.

Thus the German computer salesman, Armin Meiwes, the cannibal of Rotenburg, who challenged the legal system by pleading innocent to the dismembering and ingestion of his cyber victim on the grounds that there was no law against consensual cannibalism. In the tradition of serial killers, he wanted to satisfy his need for ultimate bonding, a kind of *über* friendship, and prowled the Internet in search of a sacrificial rite. Meiwes portrayed himself not as a killer, but as a kind of lover – a particular kind of food lover perhaps – and his prey not as a victim, but an accomplice. He was after the meal of his life.

He was inundated with passive cannibals, as it were, slavering to be eaten, and selected the one who appeared the most appetising. His choice cut, Bernd Brandes, surrendered himself quite rapturously to the pot, preening himself as the sexiest of all the candidates who clamoured to be guzzled. That sexual impulse, of a bizarre kind, underlay the act of eating is clear in the relish with which eater and eaten (lover and beloved) shared the latter's severed penis, significantly the first bit to go. Apparently it did not taste so good. It seems a shame that at least one of them was not around to savour the rest. And, of course, only one of them remained to stand trial. Meiwes was convicted of manslaughter, not murder. As the judge remarked, with commendable even-handedness, each had something to get, and each had something to give.

The Romantic in the Kitchen

There is a Romantic lurking in all of us, and it spills over into the kitchen.

It is composed of wish fulfilment, some fantasy and imagination, and letting the senses flow. It is a craving after the good and the true and the beautiful, ideally all at once, a heady if elusive dream. So Romantics value spontaneity and freshness, innocence and potential, above the constraints of formality and the disillusion of experience. Romantics are sexually driven, and are not abashed to admit it. We are all Romantics at heart, or once were. And it is in the heart, and the senses, that Romance takes root. The food lover, as one of many lovers, is a Romantic from the tip of his tongue to the base of his stomach.

Romantic impulse opens a fresh window on experience. It quickens expectation and thrives on anticipation of new promise. It contains elements of openness, eagerness and imagination, and is mercifully devoid of preconception and dead habit of mind. It expresses hunger, without indigestion. The senses are primed and unpolluted by experience, or too much of it. If it is naive, it is the kind of naivete on which experience might build, and flourish. A kind of idealism propels the romantic spirit, a sense of purpose and faith in a future. Romantics are not jaded, bored, or dead before their time. They are fired by a voracious lust for life, primarily its sensual and imaginative aspects, just as gastric juices might be said to flow when hunger is piqued, and heartbeats quicken at the sense of a lover.

I bring in hearts and gastric juices (taste and taste buds too) since minds, narrowly construed, are not enough for the Romantic spirit, they are not the full picture of the human psyche, which is a matter of yearning, a hunger for nourishment that reaches beyond the grey matter in the head. It wants blood and guts too, reaches after the visceral matter in the loins, the crevices and caverns. It is not a matter for thought and reason alone. There is passion, fantasy, inspiration, sexuality and appetite. The true cook, like the lover, is a romantic at heart, and in his belly.

Food appeals to the romantic in us, as the best meals taken with lovers attest. The aim of a romantic dinner, after all, is to translate the food into sex. The candles on the table light the way to the bedroom.

Demon Lovers

But oh! that deep romantic chasm which slanted
Down the green hill athwart a cedarn cover!
A savage place! as holy and enchanted
As e'er beneath a waning moon was haunted
By woman wailing for her demon lover!

I come out a Burgundian

One comes to cooking as a demon lover. The demonic chef is fired by the spirit of romance. For myself, I lack the discipline and exactness of the Classic cook. My cooking is hot, not cold. I eschew recipes, and lack the patience to stumble through lists of ingredients, each carefully weighed and measured. I never do the same thing twice, exactly the same. I am not anal retentive, rather cathartic. My cool Capricorn sun sign is overwhelmed by my emotive Scorpio moon and potent Uranian compulsions.

I do not measure, record and order. I prefer the casual, spontaneous flourish. Take a dollop, a knob or a dash, rather than a gram, teaspoon or measuring cup. The scales and balances are in my instinct and my taste. If I want to check I'm right, I dip my fingers into the mix and taste the flavour on my tongue. I often experiment, change in mid-stream, go off at a tangent, lose the plot. I am tempted by a sudden impulse, which might be a matter of colour or design. I know that when it looks right it will taste right. And when it tastes right to me, it is right.

Just as a distinction is drawn between the wines of Burgundy and those of Bordeaux in terms of belly (the robustness of Burgundy) and head (the finesse of Bordeaux), so with food. It is another expression of the Romantic-Classic divide. The Romantic Burgundian, as we may conceive it, cooks with, or from, the stomach, the Classical Claret is guided from the head. The first favours a certain rawness, authenticity, earthiness, and relies on instinct, spontaneity, earth and fire. The latter is classical in approach, refined, celebral, measured. Air and water. The design of the dish is constructed in the head, and its architecture is designed on the plate. It is, of course, quite possible to combine some of these elements, most cooks do, but if one were to state one's preferences for the dishes one likes most, and the restaurants one would choose, one's essential character, one way or the other, would be revealed. On this scale, I come out a Burgundian (as I am in wine).

Individuality

We are all people, come what may, but among us there are very few true individuals. People sink into the background, individuals stand out. People say yes, individuals never less than *yes, but* . . . People make lousy lovers, individuals don't. People stuff their faces, individuals cook.

Become what you are! That is the rallying cry to individuality. Come to terms with the aspiring self, which may be several selves, which is locked inside, and let it out. For the whole point about individuality is to be able to translate yourself into other lives. It is no good knowing who you are if that condemns you to terminal isolation. You may as well be dead. Your individuality needs to mingle and interact with that of others to keep it alive. You know yourself, and make sense of yourself, through others. That is the test of the true individual.

But you need to be yourself, and know what that is like, to be able to carry yourself over to other lives. Nothing will come of nothing. The more you are yourself, an individual different from others and strongly defined in yourself, the more likely you can recognise that in others, and that the connection will be reciprocal. The connection cannot be made if there is nothing to connect. Although this sounds trite, it is not as easy as it appears. We need to fight to be ourselves, and it takes longer, and is harder, than we might imagine. Most people, surely, are clones or ciphers or copies. Born originals, how come we die copies? It is important to struggle against the copy, if only to remind oneself that one is alive, and not merely breathing.

The best lessons in individuality are learned in the

kitchen and in the bedroom. Food and sex are processes that bring one out of oneself, and into the world of others. Cooking, like loving, is essentially a communal affair, it embraces and reaches out to other people. Without the participation of (at least) another, cooking becomes mere subsistence, and love is masturbation. One cooks for others, with others. A cook cooks as a lover loves.

> *Let us roll all our strength and all*
> *Our sweetness up into one ball,*
> *And tear our pleasures with rough strife*
> *Thorough the iron gates of life:*
> *Thus, though we cannot make our sun*
> *Stand still, yet we will make him run.*

I am perhaps unusual in insisting (to myself) that I bother about cooking in the way I like it, whether I am alone or not. So, on the rare occasions I am by myself, I do the whole performance, although my audience is myself. My taste buds do not change, and they appreciate the effort. I will know I have overstepped the mark when I have conversations with myself and toast my good health. For the moment, I simply eat and drink twice as much as I ordinarily would. I then bid myself a tender goodnight. It is theatre, even if the theatre of oneself.

Imagination

This is the piece of the mind that distinguishes us from other forms of life, or so we like to believe. Animals do have minds, and perhaps they can think in a certain way, but we reassure ourselves that what they cannot do is project their thoughts into another dimension: they cannot be or think anything but what they are. They are trapped in the moment, the physical reality, and cannot see the future. This is a particularly consoling thought as we are about to cut off their heads, or ram them into a pot of boiling water.

We eat animals, so we can't imagine too much about them, particularly their own imaginative capacities. Indeed, what would they think? There is a chilling story by Samuel Beckett called *Dante and the Lobster* that crystallises our unease. It ends with the reflection that plunging the lobster into boiling water is a quick and painless death. The last words are simply, 'It is not.'

For us, arrogant humans who have eclipsed the imagination for our exclusive use, imagination is what keeps us going. We are always in its thrall, whether we like it or not. Our minds are always somewhere else, or at least in more than one place or space at a time. We are thinking about tomorrow, or yesterday, or whether, or what if, or how, or perhaps ... We are infinitely whirling in possibility. We are essentially creatures of imagination. We make ourselves up as we go along. Perhaps, even, we make ourselves in the image of our fantasies.

As far as food and sex turn us on, they do so in the imagination, not only as a first necessary step, but as a sustaining illusion. Perhaps it is illusion, but if so it is a necessary one. Without imagination, there is no impulse to eat or to love, or to keep on eating or loving. We get to the experiences through an imaginative thrust, and then discover what they are.

This is a fact that appears to be rapidly forgotten or sidelined once we have got there. We conjure up the fantasy, then believe in it, translate it into reality, and lose it. Witness the dreariness and boredom of most meals and most relationships. Look at those lustreless – and lustless – eyes staring bleakly over the dining table. Those were once the eyes of love! They have lost the imaginative spark, and in so doing have lost their very purpose, motive, and animating force.

Looking around at the couples in restaurants who never say a word or catch each other's eye (or feel each other up under the table), at the couples who sleep in different beds, in different rooms ('it's your snoring, dear'), at the sullen tensions around the family dinner tables ('don't speak with your mouth full'), at the waiting rooms of the guidance counsellors and divorce lawyers ... the diagnosis is always the same. Imagination is dead (it is starving to death).

Spice up the food as much as the lovemaking! Don't put the apron on, take it off! It is no wonder housewives (do they still exist?) are bored to death. So are the husbands for whom the same unimaginative, resentful dinners are doled out, the same rumpled beds are slumped into, the same invisible children are not spoken to. Many people, apparently, would rather take a pill that contained an adequate vitamin ratio to preserve life than bother with food. It is not surprising when you look at them. They feel the same about sex, which is equally mechanical, repetitive, joyless. Imagination fails.

Toujours l'Artiste

Lovers, and lovers of food, aspire to be artists. Each succumbs to the pursuit of the beautiful. They act out of a creative, or procreative, spirit, doing it as if for the first time, as if originally, as if eternally. They want it to last for ever, and have a meaning beyond the moment. Every cook is an artist in the kitchen, just as every lover has a vision beyond himself or herself in the bedroom. Anyone who does not is simply a slave, merely going through the motions.

Nothing more dreary than the kitchen slave. You see them reflected in their shopping trolleys at the supermarket. The contents betray the spirit. Frozen dribs and drabs, precooked and predigested, tins and preservatives, instant microwave gratification, nothing fresh. The sense of resignation betrayed in the eyes of the despondent trolley slave on the way to kitchen servitude.

Each dismal night the same routine. She is bored to death, and so are the family. Half of them anorexic, the other obese. All are victims to the crap they stuff down their throats or hurl up in the toilet bowl, as if there were a subtle distinction. It certainly looks unappetising. They need to stare at the video to digest. Friday? It must be fish. Some flaky wedge frozen in a packet, suppurating in the microwave. Instant potato. Frozen vegetables. (It's no trouble.) Keep some room for the ice cream. Tomorrow it's the instant pie. Nuke it! Fill up on crisps. It's only food.

Only food. Only sex. Only art. Finally, only life. It all tastes, feels, looks the same. Dullness permeates from the kitchen to the palate, from the bedroom to the body, from the body to the spirit, the insidious odour of boredom, habit and routine.

Creativity is the word that yokes the cook to the artist. It is a matter of attitude, more than aptitude. Skills can be learned, but the spark is instinctive. If it's not, snatch it, as Prometheus did the fire. Then enter the arena of the kitchen in the spirit the artist approaches his canvas, the musician his instrument, the photographer his model. It is not what you do, remember, but how you do it. And in the *how* lies the whole difference.

We *create* a meal with something of the flair, passion, eye, and touch – the finesse – of the artist. We express in the textures and sensations of food something of what others do in words, paint or music. Music, indeed, the very food of love. A great meal is like a symphony.

We want a great meal to strike chords that are not merely sensual, but which cut deeper. We want the memory to endure. We want to make the meal unrepeatable. We are struck with a vividness in the face of truly original food that gives a little artistic frisson. For that moment, the spirit soars.

Food and Life

Food happens in a context, it is part of life. It may indeed be a way of life. How you regard food, what you do with it, and how it fits in with your scheme of things, reflects on your values and life issues. Food, and its meaning, is part of the value system of your life.

Food is the driving force of life, its prime motivator, energiser, and satisfaction. That is good enough reason to make the most of it.

Divorce food from life, and it is sheer misery, subsistence rather than living. The lonely garret, the dim light bulb, the cold silence, rattle of bones. Food comes to life with people, just as people come to life with food. A context is set up in which food is the catalyst for talk and laughter, romance, intimacy and imagination. Food enhances life, nourishes and flavours, adds piquancy, spice and colour.

We certainly spend a lot of time at it, or thinking about it, making it, shopping for it, entertaining and recovering from it. Fat people appear to think of nothing else. Our more modest focus is writ large on their chubby cheeks and bulging bottoms. Their display makes us feel guilty, of course, as if their brazenness exposes our vulnerability. That is why there are few sights as distresssing as watching fatties stuff their faces. They might have the grace to do it behind closed doors.

Food, for the fat, is life – or, equally, death. Stuff themselves to death. So full they could fall over. They read recipe books along with diet books. Food is vital to life, and should be one of its finest pleasures and accomplishments, but it is not the whole hog, so to speak. There is life after food, too.

The same is true of sex. How sex fits in with the pattern of life defines, and determines, an essential part – perhaps *the* essential part – of what we are. Food takes up more time and energy, but we are driven by sex in a way that makes it an appetite as primal as eating. As with food, we cannot do it all the time, and, like food, it palls. We can be satiated, or our palates dulled, dissatisfied or disturbed. It can also enliven us to the tips of our imagination. The fatty is like the sex maniac, the sense of proportion is skewed. Equally, the anorexic is the frigid virgin, the lonely masturbator.

Recipe Books

This is not a recipe book, although recipes, mainly of my devising, are slipped into the text. They chime with points I make, add body to the memory, make food of the thoughts. I hope they will also be used and enjoyed, for they are all deliciously simple.

I am not a professional cook, and generally I am not impressed with recipe books unless there is a quality or quirkiness to the writing that appeals. I am much more taken by the idea and the style than the content. I look for attitude. For example, I read, and reread, the admirable Elizabeth David more for her sublime prose style and élan than for her recipes. I hardly ever cook from a book, but sometimes get ideas that I can play with and adapt.

The recipes that I have made up or adapted do not claim to be startlingly original or mysterious. Many that do are not. It is the same with recipes as with jokes: there are only a few originals, everything else is variation. It is all in the execution, all in the spin. It takes flair and practice to get the edge. Differences are not in the food or the jokes, they are in the tellers and the cooks, and there is all the difference in the world. Suffering an excruciating joke is like an attack of gastritis.

Most recipe books are for duffers who really have no imagination, and often no taste. They actually loathe or

You do not eat to live. Live to eat. Fred in a Burgundy vineyard

resent cooking, and need to be told what to do in terms that are painstaking and laborious. The recipe book relieves them of the burden of imagination. That, for me, kills the experience of cooking. I want to experiment, deviate, dare. I cannot operate according to prescription, and I find the doling out of ingredients according to mass and volume too tedious to bear.

So you may well be surprised that here there are no lists of ingredients in my recipes, never mind weights and measures. But I trust you will not be put off. The recipes read casually and spontaneously, but they make perfect sense. You are guided by instinct and taste, not a measuring cup and scales. All you need to do is put enthusiasm and feeling into what you are doing, and the dishes, for the most part, look after themselves.

Remember, it is you who are the cook, and what you are creating and tasting is something of yourself. The way you do it is different from the way anyone else could. You are putting yourself on the plate, so do it with all the style, flair, and passion that comes naturally to you.

You do not eat to live. Live to eat.

Some Practical Principles

If you are to cook with pleasure – and it is otherwise not worth it (hire a cook) – then it is important to sort the basics of what you need and what you should avoid. Here is a miscellany of attitudes and accoutrements to guide you towards culinary bliss, and away from tedium.

What to have

Passion
Enthusiasm
Spontaneity

Flair
Experimentation – the kitchen, like the bedroom, is the place to live dangerously
Flexibility
Simplicity
Generosity
Attractive young helpers
Discipline
Time
Good conversation and laughter
A glass of wine in hand and a bottle open
Music
Fresh ingredients: shop on the day
Garlic
Fresh herbs
Maldon salt
Crème fraiche
Extra virgin olive oil
A couple of spoons, a skewer and a whisk
Salad dryer
Mezzaluna
Good knives
Dishcloths and oven gloves
Aga stove, if you can, otherwise gas; cooking on electricity is never as good
Five perfect copper pots, ideally procured from Dehillerin, the ultimate kitchen shop in Paris

What to discard

Prissiness, anality, uptightness, fixed ideas
Impatience, haste, short cuts
Bickering
Prima donna tantrums
Bores
Pomposity

Five perfect copper pots. Mine at the Pampoenpaleis

Vegans, New Age faddists etc
Children under the age of fifteen
Measuring cups, scales, timers etc
Recipe books
Dried herbs, flavourings, cubes, aromat etc
Frozen foods
Mouldy half-empty leftovers in fridge – what you do not eat throw away or give to your dog who will eat anything (don't be prissy here either). My noble dog Sam was as keen on pasta with wild mushrooms and crème fraiche, as he was on Thai curry, chicken carcasses, and lamb bones, but perhaps he's more goat than dog
Beer
Cigarettes
Margarine
Flavoured oils
Pre-prepared crushed garlic
The disgracefully watery slush produced by commercial dairies, masquerading as cream
Deep freeze – eat for the day
Microwave
Hostess tray
Hats and aprons – you're not a cordon bleu chef and the hat makes you look silly; splashes on clothes should be borne as trophies
All pots and pans but your five perfect ones